God's Holy Word
Is it still worth dying for?

E. G. WHITE

Remnant Publications
Coldwater MI 49036
www.remnantpublications.com

Copyright © 2008
All Rights Reserved
Printed in the USA

Published by
Remnant Publications
649 East Chicago Road
Coldwater MI 49036
517-279-1304
www.remnantpublications.com

This book is a portion of a work originally published
under the title, *The Great Controversy.*

All Bible Scripture is taken from the King James Version.

Cover design by David Berthiaume
Text design by Greg Solie • AltamontGraphics.com

ISBN 978-1-933291-42-0

Contents

One

—The Waldenses—

Amid the gloom that settled upon the earth during the long period of papal supremacy, the light of truth could not be wholly extinguished. In every age there were witnesses for God—men who cherished faith in Christ as the only mediator between God and man, who held the Bible as the only rule of life, and who hallowed the true Sabbath. How much the world owes to these men, posterity will never know. They were branded as heretics, their motives impugned, their characters maligned, their writings suppressed, misrepresented, or mutilated. Yet they stood firm, and from age to age maintained their faith in its purity, as a sacred heritage for the generations to come.

The history of God's people during the ages of darkness that followed upon Rome's supremacy is written in heaven, but they have little place in human records. Few traces of their existence can be found, except in the accusations of their persecutors. It was the policy of Rome to obliterate every trace of dissent from her doctrines or decrees. Everything heretical, whether persons or writings, she sought to destroy. Expressions of doubt, or questions as to the authority of papal dogmas, were enough to forfeit the life of rich or poor, high or low. Rome endeavored also to destroy every record of her cruelty toward dissenters. Papal councils decreed that books and writings containing such records should be committed to the flames. Before the invention of printing, books were few in number, and in a form not favorable for preservation; therefore there was little to prevent the Romanists from carrying out their purpose.

No church within the limits of Romish jurisdiction was long left undisturbed in the enjoyment of freedom of conscience. No sooner had the papacy obtained power than she stretched out her arms to crush all that refused to acknowledge her sway, and one after another the churches submitted to her dominion.

In Great Britain primitive Christianity had very early taken root. The gospel received by the Britons in the first centuries was then uncorrupted by Romish apostasy. Persecution from pagan emperors, which extended even to these far-off shores, was the only gift that the first churches of Britain received from Rome. Many of the Christians, fleeing from persecution in England, found refuge in Scotland; thence the truth was carried to Ireland, and in all these countries it was received with gladness.

When the Saxons invaded Britain, heathenism gained control. The conquerors disdained to be instructed by their slaves, and the Christians were forced to retreat to the mountains and the wild moors. Yet the light, hidden for a time, continued to burn. In Scotland, a century later, it shone out with a brightness that extended to far-distant lands. From Ireland came the pious Columba and his colaborers, who, gathering about them the scattered believers on the lonely island of Iona, made this the center of their missionary labors. Among these evangelists was an observer of the Bible Sabbath, and thus this truth was introduced among the people. A school was established at Iona, from which missionaries went out, not only to Scotland and England, but to Germany, Switzerland, and even Italy.

But Rome had fixed her eyes on Britain, and resolved to bring it under her supremacy. In the sixth century her missionaries undertook the conversion of the heathen Saxons. They were received with favor by the proud barbarians, and they induced many thousands to profess the Romish faith. As the work progressed, the papal leaders and their converts encountered the primitive Christians. A striking contrast was presented. The latter were simple, humble, and Scriptural in character, doctrine, and manners, while the former manifested the superstition, pomp, and arrogance of popery. The emissary of Rome demanded that these Christian churches acknowledge the supremacy of the sovereign pontiff. The Britons meekly replied that they desired to love all men, but that the pope was not entitled to supremacy in the church, and they could render to him only that submission which was due to every follower of Christ. Repeated attempts were made to secure their allegiance to Rome; but these humble Christians, amazed at the pride displayed by her emissaries, steadfastly replied that they knew no other master than Christ. Now the true spirit of the papacy was revealed. Said the Romish leader: "If you will not receive brethren who bring you peace, you shall receive enemies who will bring you war. If you will not unite with us in showing the Saxons the way of life, you shall receive from them the stroke of death." —J. H. Merle D'Aubigne, *History of the Reformation of the Sixteenth Century*, b. 17, ch. 2. These were no idle threats. War, intrigue, and deception were employed against these witnesses for a Bible faith, until the churches of Britain were destroyed, or forced to submit to the authority of the pope.

In lands beyond the jurisdiction of Rome there existed for many centuries bodies of Christians who remained almost wholly free from papal corruption. They were surrounded by heathenism and in the lapse of ages were affected by its errors; but they continued to regard the Bible as the only rule of faith and adhered to many of its truths. These Christians believed in the perpetuity of the law of God and observed the Sabbath of the fourth commandment. Churches that held to this faith and practice existed in Central Africa and among the Armenians of Asia.

But of those who resisted the encroachments of the papal power, the Waldenses stood foremost. In the very land where popery had fixed its seat, there its falsehood and corruption were most steadfastly resisted. For centuries the churches of Piedmont maintained their independence; but the time came at last when Rome insisted upon their submission. After ineffectual struggles against her tyranny, the leaders of these churches reluctantly acknowledged the supremacy of the power to which the whole world seemed to pay homage. There were some, however, who refused to yield to the authority of pope or prelate. They were determined to maintain their allegiance to God and to preserve the purity and simplicity of their faith. A separation took place. Those who adhered to the ancient faith now withdrew; some, forsaking their native Alps, raised the banner of truth in foreign lands; others retreated to the secluded glens and rocky fastnesses of the mountains, and there preserved their freedom to worship God.

The faith which for centuries was held and taught by the Waldensian Christians was in marked contrast to the false doctrines put forth from Rome. Their religious belief was founded upon the written word of God, the true system of Christianity. But those humble peasants, in their obscure retreats, shut away from the world, and bound to daily toil among their flocks and their vineyards, had not by themselves arrived at the truth in opposition to the dogmas and heresies of the apostate church. Theirs was not a faith newly received. Their religious belief was their inheritance from their fathers. They contended for the faith of the apostolic church,—"the faith which was once delivered unto the saints." Jude 3. "The church in the wilderness," and not the proud hierarchy enthroned in the world's great capital, was the true church of Christ, the guardian of the treasures of truth which God has committed to His people to be given to the world.

Among the leading causes that had led to the separation of the true church from Rome was the hatred of the latter toward the Bible Sabbath. As foretold by prophecy, the papal power cast down the truth to the ground. The law of God was trampled in the dust, while the traditions and customs of men were exalted. The churches that were under the rule of the papacy were early compelled to honor the Sunday as a holy day. Amid the prevailing error and superstition, many, even of the true people of God, became so bewildered that while they observed the Sabbath, they refrained from labor also on the Sunday. But this did not satisfy the papal leaders. They demanded not only that Sunday be hallowed, but that the Sabbath be profaned; and they denounced in the strongest language those who dared to show it honor. It was only by fleeing from the power of Rome that any could obey God's law in peace.

The Waldenses were among the first of the peoples of Europe to obtain a translation of the Holy Scriptures. Hundreds of years before the Reformation they possessed the Bible in manuscript in their native tongue. They had the truth unadulterated, and this rendered them the special objects of hatred and persecution. They declared the Church of Rome to be the apostate Babylon of the Apocalypse, and at the peril of their lives they stood up to resist her corruptions. While, under the pressure of long-continued persecution, some compromised their faith, little by little yielding its distinctive principles, others held fast the truth. Through ages of darkness and apostasy there were Waldenses who denied the supremacy of Rome, who rejected image worship as idolatry, and who kept the true Sabbath. Under the fiercest tempests of opposition they maintained their faith. Though gashed by the Savoyard spear, and scorched by the Romish fagot, they stood unflinchingly for God's word and His honor.

Behind the lofty bulwarks of the mountains—in all ages the refuge of the persecuted and oppressed—the Waldenses found a hiding place. Here the light of truth was kept burning amid the darkness of the Middle Ages. Here, for a thousand years, witnesses for the truth maintained the ancient faith.

God had provided for His people a sanctuary of awful grandeur, befitting the mighty truths committed to their trust. To those faithful exiles the mountains were an emblem of the immutable righteousness of Jehovah. They pointed their children to the heights towering above them in unchanging majesty, and spoke to them of Him with whom there is no variableness nor shadow of turning, whose word is as enduring as the everlasting hills. God had set fast the mountains and girded them with strength; no arm but that of Infinite Power could move them out of their place. In like manner He had established His law, the foundation of His government in heaven and upon earth. The arm of man might reach his fellow men and destroy their lives; but that arm could as readily uproot the mountains from their foundations, and hurl them into the sea, as it could change one precept of the law of Jehovah, or blot out one of His promises to those who do His will. In their fidelity to His law, God's servants should be as firm as the unchanging hills.

The mountains that girded their lowly valleys were a constant witness to God's creative power, and a never-failing assurance of His protecting care. Those pilgrims learned to love the silent symbols of Jehovah's presence. They indulged no repining because of the hardships of their lot; they were never lonely amid the mountain solitudes. They thanked God that He had provided for them an asylum from the wrath and cruelty of men. They rejoiced in their freedom to worship before Him. Often when pursued by their enemies, the strength of the hills proved a sure defense. From many a lofty cliff they chanted the praise of God, and the armies of Rome could not silence their songs of thanksgiving.

Pure, simple, and fervent was the piety of these followers of Christ. The principles of truth they valued above houses and lands, friends, kindred, even life itself. These principles they earnestly sought to impress upon the hearts of the young. From earliest childhood the youth were instructed in the Scriptures and taught to regard sacredly the claims of the law of God. Copies of the Bible were rare; therefore its precious words were committed to memory. Many were able to repeat large portions of both the Old and the New Testament. Thoughts of God were associated alike with the sublime scenery of nature and with the humble blessings of daily life. Little children learned to look with gratitude to God as the giver of every favor and every comfort.

Parents, tender and affectionate as they were, loved their children too wisely to accustom them to self-indulgence. Before them was a life of trial and hardship, perhaps a martyr's death. They were educated from childhood to endure hardness, to submit to control, and yet to think and act for themselves. Very early they were taught to bear responsibilities, to be guarded in speech, and to understand the wisdom of silence. One indiscreet word let fall in the hearing of their enemies might imperil not only the life of the speaker, but the lives of hundreds of his brethren; for as wolves hunting their prey did the enemies of truth pursue those who dared to claim freedom of religious faith.

The Waldenses had sacrificed their worldly prosperity for the truth's sake, and with persevering patience they toiled for their bread. Every spot of tillable land among the mountains was carefully improved; the valleys and the less fertile hillsides were made to yield their increase. Economy and severe self-denial formed a part of the education which the children received as their only legacy. They were taught that God designs life to be a discipline, and that their wants could be supplied only by personal labor, by forethought, care, and faith. The process was laborious and wearisome, but it was wholesome, just what man needs in his fallen state, the school which God has provided for his training and development. While the youth were inured to toil and hardship, the culture of the intellect was not neglected. They were taught that all their powers belonged to God, and that all were to be improved and developed for His service.

The Vaudois churches, in their purity and simplicity, resembled the church of apostolic times. Rejecting the supremacy of the pope and prelate, they held the Bible as the only supreme, infallible authority. Their pastors, unlike the lordly priests of Rome, followed the example of their Master, who "came not to be ministered unto, but to minister." They fed the flock of God, leading them to the green pastures and living fountains of His holy word. Far from the monuments of human pomp and pride the people assembled, not in magnificent churches or grand cathedrals, but beneath the shadow of the mountains, in the Alpine valleys, or, in time of danger, in some rocky stronghold, to listen to the words of truth from the servants of Christ. The pastors not only preached the gospel, but they visited the sick, catechized the children, admonished the erring, and labored to settle disputes and promote harmony and brotherly love. In times of peace they were sustained by the freewill offerings of the people; but, like Paul the tentmaker, each learned some trade or profession by which, if necessary, to provide for his own support.

From their pastors the youth received instruction. While attention was given to branches of general learning, the Bible was made the chief study. The Gospels of Matthew and John were committed to memory, with many of the Epistles. They were employed also in copying the Scriptures. Some manuscripts contained the whole Bible, others only brief selections, to which some simple explanations of the text were added by those who were able to expound the Scriptures. Thus were brought forth the treasures of truth so long concealed by those who sought to exalt themselves above God.

By patient, untiring labor, sometimes in the deep, dark caverns of the earth, by the light of torches, the Sacred Scriptures were written out, verse by verse, chapter by chapter. Thus the work went on, the revealed will of God shining out like pure gold; how much brighter, clearer, and more powerful because of the trials undergone for its sake only those could realize who were engaged in the work. Angels from heaven surrounded these faithful workers.

Satan had urged on the papal priests and prelates to bury the word of truth beneath the rubbish of error, heresy, and superstition; but in a most wonderful manner it was preserved uncorrupted through all the ages of darkness. It bore not the stamp of man, but the impress of God. Men have been unwearied in their efforts to obscure the plain, simple meaning of the Scriptures, and to make them contradict their own testimony; but like the ark upon the billowy deep, the word of God outrides the storms that threaten it with destruction. As the mine has rich veins of gold and silver hidden beneath the surface, so that all must dig who would discover its precious stores, so the Holy Scriptures have treasures of truth that are revealed only to the earnest, humble, prayerful seeker. God designed the Bible to be a lessonbook to all mankind, in childhood, youth, and manhood, and to be studied through all time. He gave His word to men as a revelation of Himself. Every new truth discerned is a fresh disclosure of the character of its Author. The study of the Scriptures is the means divinely ordained to bring men into closer connection with their Creator and to give them a clearer knowledge of His will. It is the medium of communication between God and man.

While the Waldenses regarded the fear of the Lord as the beginning of wisdom, they were not blind to the importance of a contact with the world, a knowledge of men and of active life, in expanding the mind and quickening the perceptions. From their schools in the mountains some of the youth were sent to institutions of learning in the cities of France or Italy, where was a more extended field for study, thought, and observation than in their native Alps. The youth thus sent forth were exposed to temptation, they witnessed vice, they encountered Satan's wily agents, who urged upon them the most subtle heresies and the most dangerous deceptions. But their education from childhood had been of a character to prepare them for all this.

In the schools whither they went, they were not to make confidants of any. Their garments were so prepared as to conceal their greatest treasure—the precious manuscripts of the Scriptures. These, the fruit of months and years of toil, they carried with them, and whenever they could do so without exciting suspicion, they cautiously placed some portion in the way of those whose hearts seemed open to receive the truth. From their mother's knee the Waldensian youth had been trained with this purpose in view; they understood their work and faithfully performed it. Converts to the true faith were won in these institutions of learning, and frequently its principles were found to be permeating the entire school; yet the papal leaders could not, by the closest inquiry, trace the so-called corrupting heresy to its source.

The spirit of Christ is a missionary spirit. The very first impulse of the renewed heart is to bring others also to the Saviour. Such was the spirit of the Vaudois Christians. They felt that God required more of them than merely to preserve the truth in its purity in their own churches; that a solemn responsibility rested upon them to let their light shine forth to those who were in darkness; by the mighty power of God's word they sought to break the bondage which Rome had imposed. The Vaudois ministers were trained as missionaries, everyone who expected to enter the ministry being required first to gain an experience as an evangelist. Each was to serve three years in some mission field before taking charge of a church at home. This service, requiring at the outset self-denial and sacrifice, was a fitting introduction to the pastor's life in those times that tried men's souls. The youth who received ordination to the sacred office saw before them, not the prospect of earthly wealth and glory, but a life of toil and danger, and possibly a martyr's fate. The missionaries went out two and two, as Jesus sent forth His disciples. With each young man was usually associated a man of age and experience, the youth being under the guidance of his companion, who was held responsible for his training, and whose instruction he was required to heed. These colaborers were not always together, but often met for prayer and counsel, thus strengthening each other in the faith.

To have made known the object of their mission would have ensured its defeat; therefore they carefully concealed their real character. Every minister possessed a knowledge of some trade or profession, and the missionaries prosecuted their work under cover of a secular calling. Usually they chose that of merchant or peddler. "They carried silks, jewelry, and other articles, at that time not easily purchasable save at distant marts; and they were welcomed as merchants where they would have been spurned as missionaries." —Wylie, b. 1, ch. 7. All the while their hearts were uplifted to God for wisdom to present a treasure more precious than gold or gems. They secretly carried about with them copies of the Bible, in whole or in part; and whenever an opportunity was presented, they called the attention of their customers to these manuscripts. Often an interest to read God's word was thus awakened, and some portion was gladly left with those who desired to receive it.

The work of these missionaries began in the plains and valleys at the foot of their own mountains, but it extended far beyond these limits. With naked feet and in garments coarse and travel-stained as were those of their Master, they passed through great cities and penetrated to distant lands. Everywhere they scattered the precious seed. Churches sprang up in their path, and the blood of martyrs witnessed for the truth. The day of God will reveal a rich harvest of souls garnered by the labors of these faithful men. Veiled and silent, the word of God was making its way through Christendom and meeting a glad reception in the homes and hearts of men.

To the Waldenses the Scriptures were not merely a record of God's dealings with men in the past, and a revelation of the responsibilities and duties of the present, but an unfolding of the perils and glories of the future. They believed that the end of all things was not far distant, and as they studied the Bible with prayer and tears they were the more deeply impressed with its precious utterances and with their duty to make known to others its saving truths. They saw the plan of salvation clearly revealed in the sacred pages, and they found comfort, hope, and peace in believing in Jesus. As the light illuminated their understanding and made glad their hearts, they longed to shed its beams upon those who were in the darkness of papal error.

They saw that under the guidance of pope and priest, multitudes were vainly endeavoring to obtain pardon by afflicting their bodies for the sin of their souls. Taught to trust to their good works to save them, they were ever looking to themselves, their minds dwelling upon their sinful condition, seeing themselves exposed to the wrath of God, afflicting soul and body, yet finding no relief. Thus conscientious souls were bound by the doctrines of Rome. Thousands abandoned friends and kindred, and spent their lives in convent cells. By oft-repeated fasts and cruel scourgings, by midnight vigils, by prostration for weary hours upon the cold, damp stones of their dreary abode, by long pilgrimages, by humiliating penance and fearful torture, thousands vainly sought to obtain peace of conscience. Oppressed with a sense of sin, and haunted with the fear of God's avenging wrath, many suffered on, until exhausted nature gave way, and without one ray of light or hope they sank into the tomb.

The Waldenses longed to break to these starving souls the bread of life, to open to them the messages of peace in the promises of God, and to point them to Christ as their only hope of salvation. The doctrine that good works can atone for the transgression of God's law they held to be based upon falsehood. Reliance upon human merit intercepts the view of Christ's infinite love. Jesus died as a sacrifice for man because the fallen race can do nothing to recommend themselves to God. The merits of a crucified and risen Saviour are the foundation of the Christian's faith. The dependence of the soul upon Christ is as real, and its connection with Him must be as close, as that of a limb to the body, or of a branch to the vine.

The teachings of popes and priests had led men to look upon the character of God, and even of Christ, as stern, gloomy, and forbidding. The Saviour was represented as so far devoid of sympathy with man in his fallen state that the mediation of priests and saints must be invoked. Those whose minds had been enlightened by the word of God longed to point these souls to Jesus as their compassionate, loving Saviour, standing with outstretched arms, inviting all to come to Him with their burden of sin, their care and weariness. They longed to clear away the obstructions which Satan had piled up that men might not see the promises, and come directly to God, confessing their sins, and obtaining pardon and peace.

Eagerly did the Vaudois missionary unfold to the inquiring mind the precious truths of the gospel. Cautiously he produced the carefully written portions of the Holy Scriptures. It was his greatest joy to give hope to the conscientious, sin-stricken soul, who could see only a God of vengeance, waiting to execute justice. With quivering lip and tearful eye did he, often on bended knees, open to his brethren the precious promises that reveal the sinner's only hope. Thus the light of truth penetrated many a darkened mind, rolling back the cloud of gloom, until the Sun of Righteousness shone into the heart with healing in His beams. It was often the case that some portion of Scripture was read again and again, the hearer desiring it to be repeated, as if he would assure himself that he had heard aright. Especially was the repetition of these words eagerly desired: "The blood of Jesus Christ His Son cleanseth us from all sin." 1 John 1:7. "As Moses lifted up the serpent in the wilderness, even so must the Son of man be lifted up: that whosoever believeth in Him should not perish, but have eternal life." John 3:14, 15.

Many were undeceived in regard to the claims of Rome. They saw how vain is the mediation of men or angels in behalf of the sinner. As the true light dawned upon their minds they exclaimed with rejoicing: "Christ is my priest; His blood is my sacrifice; His altar is my confessional." They cast themselves wholly upon the merits of Jesus, repeating the words, "Without faith it is impossible to please Him." Hebrews 11:6. "There is none other name under heaven given among men, whereby we must be saved." Acts 4:12.

The assurance of a Saviour's love seemed too much for some of these poor tempest-tossed souls to realize. So great was the relief which it brought, such a flood of light was shed upon them, that they seemed transported to heaven. Their hands were laid confidingly in the hand of Christ; their feet were planted upon the Rock of Ages. All fear of death was banished. They could now covet the prison and the fagot if they might thereby honor the name of their Redeemer.

In secret places the word of God was thus brought forth and read, sometimes to a single soul, sometimes to a little company who were longing for light and truth. Often the entire night was spent in this manner. So great would be the wonder and admiration of the listeners that the messenger of mercy was not infrequently compelled to cease his reading until the understanding could grasp the tidings of salvation. Often would words like these be uttered: "Will God indeed accept *my* offering? Will He smile upon *me*? Will He pardon *me*?" The answer was read: "Come unto Me, all ye that labor and are heavy-laden, and I will give your rest." Matthew 11:28.

Faith grasped the promise, and the glad response was heard: "No more long pilgrimages to make; no more painful journeys to holy shrines. I may come to Jesus just as I am, sinful and unholy, and He will not spurn the penitential prayer. 'Thy sins be forgiven thee.' Mine, even mine, may be forgiven!"

A tide of sacred joy would fill the heart, and the name of Jesus would be magnified by praise and thanksgiving. Those happy souls returned to their homes to diffuse light, to repeat to others, as well as they could, their new experience; that they had found the true and living Way. There was a strange and solemn power in the words of Scripture that spoke directly to the hearts of those who were longing for the truth. It was the voice of God, and it carried conviction to those who heard.

The messenger of truth went on his way; but his appearance of humility, his sincerity, his earnestness and deep fervor, were subjects of frequent remark. In many instances his hearers had not asked him whence he came or whither he went. They had been so overwhelmed, at first with surprise, and afterward with gratitude and joy, that they had not thought to question him. When they had urged him to accompany them to their homes, he had replied that he must visit the lost sheep of the flock. Could he have been an angel from heaven? they queried.

In many cases the messenger of truth was seen no more. He had made his way to other lands, or he was wearing out his life in some unknown dungeon, or perhaps his bones were whitening on the spot where he had witnessed for the truth. But the words he had left behind could not be destroyed. They were doing their work in the hearts of men; the blessed results will be fully known only in the judgment.

The Waldensian missionaries were invading the kingdom of Satan, and the powers of darkness aroused to greater vigilance. Every effort to advance the truth was watched by the prince of evil, and he excited the fears of his agents. The papal leaders saw a portent of danger to their cause from the labors of these humble itinerants. If the light of truth were allowed to shine unobstructed, it would sweep away the heavy clouds of error that enveloped the people. It would direct the minds of men to God alone and would eventually destroy the supremacy of Rome.

The very existence of this people, holding the faith of the ancient church, was a constant testimony to Rome's apostasy, and therefore excited the most bitter hatred and persecution. Their refusal to surrender the Scriptures was also an offense that Rome could not tolerate. She determined to blot them from the earth. Now began the most terrible crusades against God's people in their mountain homes. Inquisitors were put upon their track, and the scene of innocent Abel falling before the murderous Cain was often repeated.

Again and again were their fertile lands laid waste, their dwellings and chapels swept away, so that where once were flourishing fields and the homes of an innocent, industrious people, there remained only a desert. As the ravenous beast is rendered more furious by the taste of blood, so the rage of the papists was kindled to greater intensity by the sufferings of their victims. Many of these witnesses for a pure faith were pursued across the mountains and hunted down in the valleys where they were hidden, shut in by mighty forests and pinnacles of rock.

No charge could be brought against the moral character of this proscribed class. Even their enemies declared them to be a peaceable, quiet, pious people. Their grand offense was that they would not worship God according to the will of the pope. For this crime every humiliation, insult, and torture that men or devils could invent was heaped upon them.

When Rome at one time determined to exterminate the hated sect, a bull was issued by the pope, condemning them as heretics, and delivering them to slaughter. They were not accused as idlers, or dishonest, or disorderly; but it was declared that they had an appearance of piety and sanctity that seduced "the sheep of the true fold." Therefore the pope ordered "that malicious and abominable sect of malignants," if they "refuse to abjure, to be crushed like venomous snakes." —Wylie, b. 16, ch. 1. Did this haughty potentate expect to meet those words again? Did he know that they were registered in the books of heaven, to confront him at the judgment? "Inasmuch as ye have done it unto one of the least of these My brethren," said Jesus, "ye have done it unto Me." Matthew 25:40.

This bull called upon all members of the church to join the crusade against the heretics. As an incentive to engage in this cruel work, it "absolved from all ecclesiastical pains and penalties, general and particular; it released all who joined the crusade from any oaths they might have taken; it legitimatized their title to any property they might have illegally acquired; and promised remission of all their sins to such as should kill any heretic. It annulled all contracts made in favor of Vaudois, ordered their domestics to abandon them, forbade all persons to give them any aid whatever, and empowered all persons to take possession of their property." —Wylie, b. 16, ch. 1. This document clearly reveals the master spirit behind the scenes. It is the roar of the dragon, and not the voice of Christ, that is heard therein.

The papal leaders would not conform their characters to the great standard of God's law, but erected a standard to suit themselves, and determined to compel all to conform to this because Rome willed it. The most horrible tragedies were enacted. Corrupt and blasphemous priests and popes were doing the work which Satan appointed them. Mercy had no place in their natures. The same spirit that crucified Christ and slew the apostles, the same that moved the bloodthirsty Nero against the faithful in his day, was at work to rid the earth of those who were beloved of God.

The persecutions visited for many centuries upon this God-fearing people were endured by them with a patience and constancy that honored their Redeemer. Notwithstanding the crusades against them, and the inhuman butchery to which they were subjected, they continued to send out their missionaries to scatter the precious truth. They were hunted to death; yet their blood watered the seed sown, and it failed not of yielding fruit. Thus the Waldenses witnessed for God centuries before the birth of Luther. Scattered over many lands, they planted the seeds of the Reformation that began in the time of Wycliffe, grew broad and deep in the days of Luther, and is to be carried forward to the close of time by those who also are willing to suffer all things for "the word of God, and for the testimony of Jesus Christ." Revelation 1:9.

Two

—John Wycliffe—

Before the Reformation there were at times but very few copies of the Bible in existence, but God had not suffered His word to be wholly destroyed. Its truths were not to be forever hidden. He could as easily unchain the words of life as He could open prison doors and unbolt iron gates to set His servants free. In the different countries of Europe men were moved by the Spirit of God to search for the truth as for hid treasures. Providentially guided to the Holy Scriptures, they studied the sacred pages with intense interest. They were willing to accept the light at any cost to themselves. Though they did not see all things clearly, they were enabled to perceive many long-buried truths. As Heaven-sent messengers they went forth, rending asunder the chains of error and superstition, and calling upon those who had been so long enslaved, to arise and assert their liberty.

Except among the Waldenses, the word of God had for ages been locked up in languages known only to the learned; but the time had come for the Scriptures to be translated and given to the people of different lands in their native tongue. The world had passed its midnight. The hours of darkness were wearing away, and in many lands appeared tokens of the coming dawn.

In the fourteenth century arose in England the "morning star of the Reformation." John Wycliffe was the herald of reform, not for England alone, but for all Christendom. The great protest against Rome which it was permitted him to utter was never to be silenced. That protest opened the struggle which was to result in the emancipation of individuals, of churches, and of nations.

Wycliffe received a liberal education, and with him the fear of the Lord was the beginning of wisdom. He was noted at college for his fervent piety as well as for his remarkable talents and sound scholarship. In his thirst for knowledge he sought to become acquainted with every branch of learning. He was educated in the scholastic philosophy, in the canons of the church, and in the civil law, especially that of his own country. In his after labors the value of this early training was apparent. A thorough acquaintance with the speculative philosophy of his time enabled him to expose its errors; and by his study of national and ecclesiastical law he was prepared to engage in the great struggle for civil and religious liberty. While he could wield the weapons drawn from the word of God, he had acquired the intellectual discipline of the schools, and he understood the tactics of the schoolmen. The power of his genius and the extent and thoroughness of his knowledge commanded the respect of both friends and foes. His adherents saw with satisfaction that their champion stood foremost among the leading minds of the nation; and his enemies were prevented from casting contempt upon the cause of reform by exposing the ignorance or weakness of its supporter.

While Wycliffe was still at college, he entered upon the study of the Scriptures. In those early times, when the Bible existed only in the ancient languages, scholars were enabled to find their way to the fountain of truth, which was closed to the uneducated classes. Thus already the way had been prepared for Wycliffe's future work as a Reformer. Men of learning had studied the word of God and had found the great truth of His free grace there revealed. In their teachings they had spread a knowledge of this truth, and had led others to turn to the living oracles.

When Wycliffe's attention was directed to the Scriptures, he entered upon their investigation with the same thoroughness which had enabled him to master the learning of the schools. Heretofore he had felt a great want, which neither his scholastic studies nor the teaching of the church could satisfy. In the word of God he found that which he had before sought in vain. Here he saw the plan of salvation revealed and Christ set forth as the only advocate for man. He gave himself to the service of Christ and determined to proclaim the truths he had discovered.

Like after Reformers, Wycliffe did not, at the opening of his work, foresee whither it would lead him. He did not set himself deliberately in opposition to Rome. But devotion to truth could not but bring him in conflict with falsehood. The more clearly he discerned the errors of the papacy, the more earnestly he presented the teaching of the Bible. He saw that Rome had forsaken the word of God for human tradition; he fearlessly accused the priesthood of having banished the Scriptures, and demanded that the Bible be restored to the people and that its authority be again established in the church. He was an able and earnest teacher and an eloquent preacher, and his daily life was a demonstration of the truths he preached. His knowledge of the Scriptures, the force of his reasoning, the purity of his life, and his unbending courage and integrity won for him general esteem and confidence. Many of the people had become dissatisfied with their former faith as they saw the iniquity that prevailed in the Roman Church, and they hailed with unconcealed joy the truths brought to view by Wycliffe; but the papal leaders were filled with rage when they perceived that this Reformer was gaining an influence greater than their own.

Wycliffe was a keen detector of error, and he struck fearlessly against many of the abuses sanctioned by the authority of Rome. While acting as chaplain for the king, he took a bold stand against the payment of tribute claimed by the pope from the English monarch and showed that the papal assumption of authority over secular rulers was contrary to both reason and revelation. The demands of the pope had excited great indignation, and Wycliffe's teachings exerted an influence upon the leading minds of the nation. The king and the nobles united in denying the pontiff's claim to temporal authority and in refusing the payment of the tribute. Thus an effectual blow was struck against the papal supremacy in England.

Another evil against which the Reformer waged long and resolute battle was the institution of the orders of mendicant friars. These friars swarmed in England, casting a blight upon the greatness and prosperity of the nation. Industry, education, morals, all felt the withering influence. The monk's life of idleness and beggary was not only a heavy drain upon the resources of the people, but it brought useful labor into contempt. The youth were demoralized and corrupted. By the influence of the friars many were induced to enter a cloister and devote themselves to a monastic life, and this not only without the consent of their parents, but even without their knowledge and contrary to their commands. One of the early Fathers of the Roman Church, urging the claims of monasticism above the obligations of filial love and duty, had declared: "Though thy father should lie before thy door weeping and lamenting, and thy mother should show the body that bore thee and the breasts that nursed thee, see that thou trample them underfoot, and go onward straightway to Christ." By this "monstrous inhumanity," as Luther afterward styled it, "savoring more of the wolf and the tyrant than of the Christian and the man," were the hearts of children steeled against their parents. —Barnas Sears, *The Life of Luther*, pages 70, 69. Thus did the papal leaders, like the Pharisees of old, make the commandment of God of none effect by their tradition. Thus homes were made desolate and parents were deprived of the society of their sons and daughters.

Even the students in the universities were deceived by the false representations of the monks and induced to join their orders. Many afterward repented this step, seeing that they had blighted their own lives and had brought sorrow upon their parents; but once fast in the snare it was impossible for them to obtain their freedom. Many parents, fearing the influence of the monks, refused to send their sons to the universities. There was a marked falling off in the number of students in attendance at the great centers of learning. The schools languished, and ignorance prevailed.

The pope had bestowed on these monks the power to hear confessions and to grant pardon. This became a source of great evil. Bent on enhancing their gains, the friars were so ready to grant absolution that criminals of all descriptions resorted to them, and, as a result, the worst vices rapidly increased. The sick and the poor were left to suffer, while the gifts that should have relieved their wants went to the monks, who with threats demanded the alms of the people, denouncing the impiety of those who should withhold gifts from their orders. Notwithstanding their profession of poverty, the wealth of the friars was constantly increasing, and their magnificent edifices and luxurious tables made more apparent the growing poverty of the nation. And while spending their time in luxury and pleasure, they sent out in their stead ignorant men, who could only recount marvelous tales, legends, and jests to amuse the people and make them still more completely the dupes of the monks. Yet the friars continued to maintain their hold on the superstitious multitudes and led them to believe that all religious duty was comprised in acknowledging the supremacy of the pope, adoring the saints, and making gifts to the monks, and that this was sufficient to secure them a place in heaven.

Men of learning and piety had labored in vain to bring about a reform in these monastic orders; but Wycliffe, with clearer insight, struck at the root of the evil, declaring that the system itself was false and that it should be abolished. Discussion and inquiry were awakening. As the monks traversed the country, vending the pope's pardons, many were led to doubt the possibility of purchasing forgiveness with money, and they questioned whether they should not seek pardon from God rather than from the pontiff of Rome. Not a few were alarmed at the rapacity of the friars, whose greed seemed never to be satisfied. "The monks and priests of Rome," said they, "are eating us away like a cancer. God must deliver us, or the people will perish." —D'Aubigne, b. 17, ch. 7. To cover their avarice, these begging monks claimed that they were following the Saviour's example, declaring that Jesus and His disciples had been supported by the charities of the people. This claim resulted in injury to their cause, for it led many to the Bible to learn the truth for themselves—a result which of all others was least desired by Rome. The minds of men were directed to the Source of truth, which it was her object to conceal.

Wycliffe began to write and publish tracts against the friars, not, however, seeking so much to enter into dispute with them as to call the minds of the people to the teachings of the Bible and its Author. He declared that the power of pardon or of excommunication is possessed by the pope in no greater degree than by common priests, and that no man can be truly excommunicated unless he has first brought upon himself the condemnation of God. In no more effectual way could he have undertaken the overthrow of that mammoth fabric of spiritual and temporal dominion which the pope had erected and in which the souls and bodies of millions were held captive.

Again Wycliffe was called to defend the rights of the English crown against the encroachments of Rome; and being appointed a royal ambassador, he spent two years in the Netherlands, in conference with the commissioners of the pope. Here he was brought into communication with ecclesiastics from France,

Italy, and Spain, and he had an opportunity to look behind the scenes and gain a knowledge of many things which would have remained hidden from him in England. He learned much that was to give point to his after labors. In these representatives from the papal court he read the true character and aims of the hierarchy. He returned to England to repeat his former teachings more openly and with greater zeal, declaring that covetousness, pride, and deception were the gods of Rome.

In one of his tracts he said, speaking of the pope and his collectors: "They draw out of our land poor men's livelihood, and many thousand marks, by the year, of the king's money, for sacraments and spiritual things, that is cursed heresy of simony, and maketh all Christendom assent and maintain this heresy. And certes though our realm had a huge hill of gold, and never other man took thereof but only this proud worldly priest's collector, by process of time this hill must be spended; for he taketh ever money out of our land, and sendeth nought again but God's curse for his simony." —John Lewis, *History of the Life and Sufferings of J. Wiclif*, page 37.

Soon after his return to England, Wycliffe received from the king the appointment to the rectory of Lutterworth. This was an assurance that the monarch at least had not been displeased by his plain speaking. Wycliffe's influence was felt in shaping the action of the court, as well as in molding the belief of the nation.

The papal thunders were soon hurled against him. Three bulls were dispatched to England,—to the university, to the king, and to the prelates,—all commanding immediate and decisive measures to silence the teacher of heresy. (Augustus Neander, *General History of the Christian Religion and Church*, period 6, sec. 2, pt. 1, par. 8.) Before the arrival of the bulls, however, the bishops, in their zeal, had summoned Wycliffe before them for trial. But two of the most powerful princes in the kingdom accompanied him to the tribunal; and the people, surrounding the building and rushing in, so intimidated the judges that the proceedings were for the time suspended, and he was allowed to go his way in peace. A little later, Edward III, whom in his old age the prelates were seeking to influence against the Reformer, died, and Wycliffe's former protector became regent of the kingdom.

But the arrival of the papal bulls laid upon all England a peremptory command for the arrest and imprisonment of the heretic. These measures pointed directly to the stake. It appeared certain that Wycliffe must soon fall a prey to the vengeance of Rome. But He who declared to one of old, "Fear not: ... I am thy shield" (Genesis 15:1), again stretched out His hand to protect His servant. Death came, not to the Reformer, but to the pontiff who had decreed his destruction. Gregory XI died, and the ecclesiastics who had assembled for Wycliffe's trial, dispersed.

God's providence still further overruled events to give opportunity for the growth of the Reformation. The death of Gregory was followed by the election of two rival popes. Two conflicting powers, each professedly infallible, now claimed obedience. Each called upon the faithful to assist him in making war upon the other, enforcing his demands by terrible anathemas against his adversaries, and promises of rewards in heaven to his supporters. This occurrence greatly weakened the power of the papacy. The rival factions had all they could do to attack each other, and Wycliffe for a time had rest. Anathemas and recriminations were flying from pope to pope, and torrents of blood were poured out to support their conflicting claims. Crimes and scandals flooded the church. Meanwhile the Reformer, in the quiet retirement of his parish of Lutterworth, was laboring diligently to point men from the contending popes to Jesus, the Prince of Peace.

The schism, with all the strife and corruption which it caused, prepared the way for the Reformation by enabling the people to see what the papacy really was. In a tract which he published, *On the Schism of the Popes*, Wycliffe called upon the people to consider whether these two priests were not speaking the truth in condemning each other as the anti-christ. "God," said he, "would no longer suffer the fiend to reign in only one such priest, but . . . made division among two, so that men, in Christ's name, may the more easily overcome them both." —R. Vaughan, *Life and Opinions of John de Wycliffe*, vol. 2, p. 6.

Wycliffe, like his Master, preached the gospel to the poor. Not content with spreading the light in their humble homes in his own parish of Lutterworth, he determined that it should be carried to every part of England. To accomplish this he organized a body of preachers, simple, devout men, who loved the truth and desired nothing so much as to extend it. These men went everywhere, teaching in the market places, in the streets of the great cities, and in the country lanes. They sought out the aged, the sick, and the poor, and opened to them the glad tidings of the grace of God.

As a professor of theology at Oxford, Wycliffe preached the word of God in the halls of the university. So faithfully did he present the truth to the students under his instruction, that he received the title of "the gospel doctor." But the greatest work of his life was to be the translation of the Scriptures into the English language. In a work, *On the Truth and Meaning of Scripture*, he expressed his intention to translate the Bible, so that every man in England might read, in the language in which he was born, the wonderful works of God.

But suddenly his labors were stopped. Though not yet sixty years of age, unceasing toil, study, and the assaults of his enemies had told upon his strength and made him prematurely old. He was attacked by a dangerous illness. The tidings brought great joy to the friars. Now they thought he would bitterly repent the evil he had done the church, and they hurried to his chamber to listen to his confession. Representatives from the four religious orders, with four civil officers, gathered about the supposed dying man. "You have death on your lips," they said; "be touched by your faults, and retract in our presence all that you have said to our injury." The Reformer listened in silence; then he bade his attendant raise him in his bed, and, gazing steadily upon them as they stood waiting for his recantation, he said, in the firm, strong voice which had so often caused them to tremble: "I shall not die, but live; and again declare the evil deeds of the friars." —D'Aubigne, b. 17, ch. 7. Astonished and abashed, the monks hurried from the room.

Wycliffe's words were fulfilled. He lived to place in the hands of his country-men the most powerful of all weapons against Rome—to give them the Bible, the Heaven-appointed agent to liberate, enlighten, and evangelize the people. There were many and great obstacles to surmount in the accomplishment of this work. Wycliffe was weighed down with infirmities; he knew that only a few years for labor remained for him; he saw the opposition which he must meet; but, encouraged by the promises of God's word, he went forward nothing daunted. In the full vigor of his intellectual powers, rich in experience, he had been preserved and prepared by God's special providence for this, the greatest of his labors. While all Christendom was filled with tumult, the Reformer in his rectory at Lutterworth, unheeding the storm that raged without, applied himself to his chosen task.

At last the work was completed—the first English translation of the Bible ever made. The word of God was opened to England. The Reformer feared not now the prison or the stake. He had placed in the hands of the English people a light which should never be extinguished. In giving the Bible to his countrymen, he had done more to break the fetters of ignorance and vice, more to liberate and elevate his country, than was ever achieved by the most brilliant victories on fields of battle.

The art of printing being still unknown, it was only by slow and wearisome labor that copies of the Bible could be multiplied. So great was the interest to obtain the book, that many willingly engaged in the work of transcribing it, but it was with difficulty that the copyists could supply the demand. Some of the more wealthy purchasers desired the whole Bible. Others bought only a portion. In many cases, several families united to purchase a copy. Thus Wycliffe's Bible soon found its way to the homes of the people.

The appeal to men's reason aroused them from their passive submission to papal dogmas. Wycliffe now taught the distinctive doctrines of Protestantism—salvation through faith in Christ, and the sole infallibility of the Scriptures. The preachers whom he had sent out circulated the Bible, together with the Reformer's writings, and with such success that the new faith was accepted by nearly one half of the people of England.

The appearance of the Scriptures brought dismay to the authorities of the church. They had now to meet an agency more powerful than Wycliffe—an agency against which their weapons would avail little. There was at this time no law in England prohibiting the Bible, for it had never before been published in the language of the people. Such laws were afterward enacted and rigorously enforced. Meanwhile, notwithstanding the efforts of the priests, there was for a season opportunity for the circulation of the word of God.

Again the papal leaders plotted to silence the Reformer's voice. Before three tribunals he was successively summoned for trial, but without avail. First a synod of bishops declared his writings heretical, and, winning the young king, Richard II, to their side, they obtained a royal decree consigning to prison all who should hold the condemned doctrines.

Wycliffe appealed from the synod to Parliament; he fearlessly arraigned the hierarchy before the national council and demanded a reform of the enormous abuses sanctioned by the church. With convincing power he portrayed the usurpation and corruptions of the papal see. His enemies were brought to confusion. The friends and supporters of Wycliffe had been forced to yield, and it had been confidently expected that the Reformer himself, in his old age, alone and friendless, would bow to the combined authority of the crown and the miter. But instead of this the papists saw themselves defeated. Parliament, roused by the stirring appeals of Wycliffe, repealed the persecuting edict, and the Reformer was again at liberty.

A third time he was brought to trial, and now before the highest ecclesiastical tribunal in the kingdom. Here no favor would be shown to heresy. Here at last Rome would triumph, and the Reformer's work would be stopped. So thought the papists. If they could but accomplish their purpose, Wycliffe would be forced to abjure his doctrines, or would leave the court only for the flames.

But Wycliffe did not retract; he would not dissemble. He fearlessly maintained his teachings and repelled the accusations of his persecutors. Losing sight of himself, of his position, of the occasion, he summoned his hearers before the divine tribunal, and weighed their sophistries and deceptions in the balances of eternal truth. The power of the Holy Spirit was felt in the council room. A spell from God was upon the hearers. They seemed to have no power to leave the place. As arrows from the Lord's quiver, the Reformer's words pierced their hearts. The charge of heresy, which they had brought against him, he with convincing power threw back upon themselves. Why, he demanded, did they dare to spread their errors? For the sake of gain, to make merchandise of the grace of God?

"With whom, think you," he finally said, "are ye contending? with an old man on the brink of the grave? No! with Truth—Truth which is stronger than you, and will overcome you." —Wylie, b. 2, ch. 13. So saying, he withdrew from the assembly, and not one of his adversaries attempted to prevent him.

Wycliffe's work was almost done; the banner of truth which he had so long borne was soon to fall from his hand; but once more he was to bear witness for the gospel. The truth was to be proclaimed from the very stronghold of the kingdom of error. Wycliffe was summoned for trial before the papal tribunal at Rome, which had so often shed the blood of the saints. He was not blind to the danger that threatened him, yet he would have obeyed the summons had not a shock of palsy made it impossible for him to perform the journey. But though his voice was not to be heard at Rome, he could speak by letter, and this he determined to do. From his rectory the Reformer wrote to the pope a letter, which, while respectful in tone and Christian in spirit, was a keen rebuke to the pomp and pride of the papal see.

"Verily I do rejoice," he said, "to open and declare unto every man the faith which I do hold, and especially unto the bishop of Rome: which, forasmuch as I do suppose to be sound and true, he will most willingly confirm my said faith, or if it be erroneous, amend the same.

"First, I suppose that the gospel of Christ is the whole body of God's law. … I do give and hold the bishop of Rome, forasmuch as he is the vicar of Christ here on earth, to be most bound, of all other men, unto that law of the gospel. For the greatness among Christ's disciples did not consist in worldly dignity or honors, but in the near and exact following of Christ in His life and manners. … Christ, for the time of His pilgrimage here, was a most poor man, abjecting and casting off all worldly rule and honor. …

"No faithful man ought to follow either the pope himself or any of the holy men, but in such points as he hath followed the Lord Jesus Christ; for Peter and the sons of Zebedee, by desiring worldly honor, contrary to the following of Christ's steps, did offend, and therefore in those errors they are not to be followed. …

"The pope ought to leave unto the secular power all temporal dominion and rule, and thereunto effectually to move and exhort his whole clergy; for so did Christ, and especially by His apostles. Wherefore, if I have erred in any of these points, I will most humbly submit myself unto correction, even by death, if necessity so require; and if I could labor according to my will or desire in mine own person, I would surely present myself before the bishop of Rome; but the Lord hath otherwise visited me to the contrary, and hath taught me rather to obey God than men."

In closing he said: "Let us pray unto our God, that He will so stir up our Pope Urban VI, as he began, that he with his clergy may follow the Lord Jesus Christ in life and manners; and that they may teach the people effectually, and that they, likewise, may faithfully follow them in the same." —John Foxe, *Acts and Monuments*, vol. 3, pp. 49, 50.

Thus Wycliffe presented to the pope and his cardinals the meekness and humility of Christ, exhibiting not only to themselves but to all Christendom the contrast between them and the Master whose representatives they professed to be.

Wycliffe fully expected that his life would be the price of his fidelity. The king, the pope, and the bishops were united to accomplish his ruin, and it seemed certain that a few months at most would bring him to the stake. But his courage was unshaken. "Why do you talk of seeking the crown of martyrdom afar?" he said. "Preach the gospel of Christ to haughty prelates, and martyrdom will not fail you. What! I should live and be silent? … Never! Let the blow fall, I await its coming." —D'Aubigne, b. 17, ch. 8.

But God's providence still shielded His servant. The man who for a whole lifetime had stood boldly in defense of the truth, in daily peril of his life, was not to fall a victim of the hatred of its foes. Wycliffe had never sought to shield himself, but the Lord had been his protector; and now, when his enemies felt sure of their prey, God's hand removed him beyond their reach. In his church at Lutterworth, as he was about to dispense the communion, he fell, stricken with palsy, and in a short time yielded up his life.

God had appointed to Wycliffe his work. He had put the word of truth in his mouth, and He set a guard about him that this word might come to the people. His life was protected, and his labors were prolonged, until a foundation was laid for the great work of the Reformation.

Wycliffe came from the obscurity of the Dark Ages. There were none who went before him from whose work he could shape his system of reform. Raised up like John the Baptist to accomplish a special mission, he was the herald of a new era. Yet in the system of truth which he presented there was a unity and completeness which Reformers who followed him did not exceed, and which some did not reach, even a hundred years later. So broad and deep was laid the foundation, so firm and true was the framework, that it needed not to be reconstructed by those who came after him.

The great movement that Wycliffe inaugurated, which was to liberate the conscience and the intellect, and set free the nations so long bound to the triumphal car of Rome, had its spring in the Bible. Here was the source of that stream of blessing, which, like the water of life, has flowed down the ages since the fourteenth century. Wycliffe accepted the Holy Scriptures with implicit faith as the inspired revelation of God's will, a sufficient rule of faith and practice. He had been educated to regard the Church of Rome as the divine, infallible authority, and to accept with unquestioning reverence the established teachings and customs of a thousand years; but he turned away from all these to listen to God's holy word. This was the authority which he urged the people to acknowledge. Instead of the church speaking through the pope, he declared the only true authority to be the voice of God speaking through His word. And he taught not only that the Bible is a perfect revelation of God's will, but that the Holy Spirit is its only interpreter, and that every man is, by the study of its teachings, to learn his duty for himself. Thus he turned the minds of men from the pope and the Church of Rome to the word of God.

Wycliffe was one of the greatest of the Reformers. In breadth of intellect, in clearness of thought, in firmness to maintain the truth, and in boldness to defend it, he was equaled by few who came after him. Purity of life, unwearying diligence in study and in labor, incorruptible integrity, and Christlike love and faithfulness in his ministry, characterized the first of the Reformers. And this notwithstanding the intellectual darkness and moral corruption of the age from which he emerged.

The character of Wycliffe is a testimony to the educating, transforming power of the Holy Scriptures. It was the Bible that made him what he was. The effort to grasp the great truths of revelation imparts freshness and vigor to all the faculties. It expands the mind, sharpens the perceptions, and ripens the judgment. The study of the Bible will ennoble every thought, feeling, and aspiration as no other study can. It gives stability of purpose, patience, courage, and fortitude; it refines the character and sanctifies the soul. An earnest, reverent study of the Scriptures, bringing the mind of the student in direct contact with the infinite mind, would give to the world men of stronger and more active intellect, as well as of nobler principle, than has ever resulted from the ablest training that human philosophy affords. "The entrance of Thy words," says the psalmist, "giveth light; it giveth understanding." Psalm 119:130.

The doctrines which had been taught by Wycliffe continued for a time to spread; his followers, known as Wycliffites and Lollards, not only traversed England, but scattered to other lands, carrying the knowledge of the gospel. Now that their leader was removed, the preachers labored with even greater zeal than before, and multitudes flocked to listen to their teachings. Some of the nobility, and even the wife of the king, were among the converts. In many places there was a marked reform in the manners of the people, and the idolatrous symbols of Romanism were removed from the churches. But soon the pitiless storm of persecution burst upon those who had dared to accept the Bible as their guide. The English monarchs, eager to strengthen their power by securing the support of Rome, did not hesitate to sacrifice the Reformers. For the first time in the history of England the stake was decreed against the disciples of the gospel. Martyrdom succeeded martyrdom. The advocates of truth, proscribed and tortured, could only pour their cries into the ear of the Lord of Sabaoth. Hunted as foes of the church and traitors to the realm, they continued to preach in secret places, finding shelter as best they could in the humble homes of the poor, and often hiding away even in dens and caves.

Notwithstanding the rage of persecution, a calm, devout, earnest, patient protest against the prevailing corruption of religious faith continued for centuries to be uttered. The Christians of that early time had only a partial knowledge of the truth, but they had learned to love and obey God's word, and they patiently suffered for its sake. Like the disciples in apostolic days, many sacrificed their worldly possessions for the cause of Christ. Those who were permitted to dwell in their homes gladly sheltered their banished brethren, and when they too were driven forth they cheerfully accepted the lot of the outcast. Thousands, it is true, terrified by the fury of their persecutors, purchased their freedom at the sacrifice of their faith, and went out of their prisons, clothed in penitents' robes, to publish their recantation. But the number was not small—and among them were men of noble birth as well as the humble and lowly—who bore fearless testimony to the truth in dungeon cells, in "Lollard towers," and in the midst of torture and flame, rejoicing that they were counted worthy to know "the fellowship of His sufferings."

The papists had failed to work their will with Wycliffe during his life, and their hatred could not be satisfied while his body rested quietly in the grave. By the decree of the Council of Constance, more than forty years after his death his bones were exhumed and publicly burned, and the ashes were thrown into a neighboring brook. "This brook," says an old writer, "hath conveyed his ashes into Avon, Avon into Severn, Severn into the narrow seas, they into the main ocean. And thus the ashes of Wycliffe are the emblem of his doctrine, which now is dispersed all the world over." —T. Fuller, *Church History of Britain*, b. 4, sec. 2, par. 54. Little did his enemies realize the significance of their malicious act.

It was through the writings of Wycliffe that John Huss, of Bohemia, was led to renounce many of the errors of Romanism and to enter upon the work of reform. Thus in these two countries, so widely separated, the seed of truth was sown. From Bohemia the work extended to other lands. The minds of men were directed to the long-forgotten word of God. A divine hand was preparing the way for the Great Reformation.

Three

—Huss and Jerome—

T he gospel had been planted in Bohemia as early as the ninth century. The Bible was translated, and public worship was conducted, in the language of the people. But as the power of the pope increased, so the word of God was obscured. Gregory VII, who had taken it upon himself to humble the pride of kings, was no less intent upon enslaving the people, and accordingly a bull was issued forbidding public worship to be conducted in the Bohemian tongue. The pope declared that "it was pleasing to the Omnipotent that His worship should be celebrated in an unknown language, and that many evils and heresies had arisen from not observing this rule." —Wylie, b. 3, ch. 1. Thus Rome decreed that the light of God's word should be extinguished and the people should be shut up in darkness. But Heaven had provided other agencies for the preservation of the church. Many of the Waldenses and Albigenses, driven by persecution from their homes in France and Italy, came to Bohemia. Though they dared not teach openly, they labored zealously in secret. Thus the true faith was preserved from century to century.

Before the days of Huss there were men in Bohemia who rose up to condemn openly the corruption in the church and the profligacy of the people. Their labors excited widespread interest. The fears of the hierarchy were roused, and persecution was opened against the disciples of the gospel. Driven to worship in the forests and the mountains, they were hunted by soldiers, and many were put to death. After a time it was decreed that all who departed from the Romish worship should be burned. But while the Christians yielded up their lives, they looked forward to the triumph of their cause. One of those who "taught that salvation was only to be found by faith in the crucified Saviour," declared when dying: "The rage of the enemies of the truth now prevails against us, but it will not be forever; there shall arise one from among the common people, without sword or authority, and against him they shall not be able to prevail." —*Ibid.*, b. 3, ch. 1. Luther's time was yet far distant; but already one was rising, whose testimony against Rome would stir the nations.

John Huss was of humble birth, and was early left an orphan by the death of his father. His pious mother, regarding education and the fear of God as the most valuable of possessions, sought to secure this heritage for her son. Huss studied at the provincial school, and then repaired to the university at Prague, receiving admission as a charity scholar. He was accompanied on the journey to Prague by his mother; widowed and poor, she had no gifts of worldly wealth to bestow upon her son, but as they drew near to the great city, she kneeled down beside the fatherless youth and invoked for him the blessing of their Father in heaven. Little did that mother realize how her prayer was to be answered.

At the university, Huss soon distinguished himself by his untiring application and rapid progress, while his blameless life and gentle, winning deportment gained him universal esteem. He was a sincere adherent of the Roman Church and an earnest seeker for the spiritual blessings which it professes to bestow. On the occasion of a jubilee he went to confession, paid the last few coins in his scanty store, and joined in the processions, that he might share in the absolution promised. After completing his college course, he entered the priesthood, and rapidly attaining to eminence, he soon became attached to the court of the king. He was also made professor and afterward rector of the university where he had received his education. In a few years the humble charity scholar had become the pride of his country, and his name was renowned throughout Europe.

But it was in another field that Huss began the work of reform. Several years after taking priest's orders he was appointed preacher of the chapel of Bethlehem. The founder of this chapel had advocated, as a matter of great importance, the preaching of the Scriptures in the language of the people. Notwithstanding Rome's opposition to this practice, it had not been wholly discontinued in Bohemia. But there was great ignorance of the Bible, and the worst vices prevailed among the people of all ranks. These evils Huss unsparingly denounced, appealing to the word of God to enforce the principles of truth and purity which he inculcated.

A citizen of Prague, Jerome, who afterward became so closely associated with Huss, had, on returning from England, brought with him the writings of Wycliffe. The queen of England, who had been a convert to Wycliffe's teachings, was a Bohemian princess, and through her influence also the Reformer's works were widely circulated in her native country. These works Huss read with interest; he believed their author to be a sincere Christian and was inclined to regard with favor the reforms which he advocated. Already, though he knew it not, Huss had entered upon a path which was to lead him far away from Rome.

About this time there arrived in Prague two strangers from England, men of learning, who had received the light and had come to spread it in this distant land. Beginning with an open attack on the pope's supremacy, they were soon silenced by the authorities; but being unwilling to relinquish their purpose, they had recourse to other measures. Being artists as well as preachers, they proceeded to exercise their skill. In a place open to the public they drew two pictures. One represented the entrance of Christ into Jerusalem, "meek, and sitting upon an ass" (Matthew 21:5), and followed by His disciples in travel-worn garments and with naked feet. The other picture portrayed a pontifical procession—the pope arrayed in his rich robes and triple crown, mounted upon a horse magnificently adorned, preceded by trumpeters and followed by cardinals and prelates in dazzling array.

Here was a sermon which arrested the attention of all classes. Crowds came to gaze upon the drawings. None could fail to read the moral, and many were deeply impressed by the contrast between the meekness and humility of Christ the Master and the pride and arrogance of the pope, His professed servant. There was great commotion in Prague, and the strangers after a time found it necessary, for their own safety, to depart. But the lesson they had taught was not forgotten. The pictures made a deep impression on the mind of Huss and led him to a closer study of the Bible and of Wycliffe's writings. Though he was not prepared, even yet, to accept all the reforms advocated by Wycliffe, he saw more clearly the true character of the papacy, and with greater zeal denounced the pride, the ambition, and the corruption of the hierarchy.

From Bohemia the light extended to Germany, for disturbances in the University of Prague caused the withdrawal of hundreds of German students. Many of them had received from Huss their first knowledge of the Bible, and on their return they spread the gospel in their fatherland.

Tidings of the work at Prague were carried to Rome, and Huss was soon summoned to appear before the pope. To obey would be to expose himself to certain death. The king and queen of Bohemia, the university, members of the nobility, and officers of the government united in an appeal to the pontiff that Huss be permitted to remain at Prague and to answer at Rome by deputy. Instead of granting this request, the pope proceeded to the trial and condemnation of Huss, and then declared the city of Prague to be under interdict.

In that age this sentence, whenever pronounced, created widespread alarm. The ceremonies by which it was accompanied were well adapted to strike terror to a people who looked upon the pope as the representative of God Himself, holding the keys of heaven and hell, and possessing power to invoke temporal as well as spiritual judgments. It was believed that the gates of heaven were closed against the region smitten with interdict; that until it should please the pope to remove the ban, the dead were shut out from the abodes of bliss. In token of this terrible calamity, all the services of religion were suspended. The churches were closed. Marriages were solemnized in the churchyard. The dead, denied burial in consecrated ground, were interred, without the rites of sepulture, in the ditches or the fields. Thus by measures which appealed to the imagination, Rome essayed to control the consciences of men.

The city of Prague was filled with tumult. A large class denounced Huss as the cause of all their calamities and demanded that he be given up to the vengeance of Rome. To quiet the storm, the Reformer withdrew for a time to his native village. Writing to the friends whom he had left at Prague, he said: "If I have withdrawn from the midst of you, it is to follow the precept and example of Jesus Christ, in order not to give room to the ill-minded to draw on themselves eternal condemnation, and in order not to be to the pious a cause of affliction and persecution. I have retired also through an apprehension that impious priests might continue for a longer time to prohibit the preaching of the word of God amongst you; but I have not quitted you to deny the divine truth, for which, with God's assistance, I am willing to die." —Bonnechose, *The Reformers Before the Reformation*, vol. 1, p. 87. Huss did not cease his labors, but traveled through the surrounding country, preaching to eager crowds. Thus the measures to which the pope resorted to suppress the gospel were causing it to be the more widely extended. "We can do nothing against the truth, but for the truth." 2 Corinthians 13:8.

"The mind of Huss, at this stage of his career, would seem to have been the scene of a painful conflict. Although the church was seeking to overwhelm him by her thunderbolts, he had not renounced her authority. The Roman Church was still to him the spouse of Christ, and the pope was the representative and vicar of God. What Huss was warring against was the abuse of authority, not the principle itself. This brought on a terrible conflict between the convictions of his understanding and the claims of his conscience. If the authority was just and infallible, as he believed it to be, how came it that he felt compelled to disobey it? To obey, he saw, was to sin; but why should obedience to an infallible church lead to such an issue? This was the problem he could not solve; this was the doubt that tortured him hour by hour. The nearest approximation to a solution which he was able to make was that it had happened again, as once before in the days of the Saviour, that the priests of the church had become wicked persons and were using their lawful authority for unlawful ends. This led him to adopt for his own guidance, and to preach to others for theirs, the maxim that the precepts of Scripture, conveyed through the understanding, are to rule the conscience; in other words, that God speaking in the Bible, and not the church speaking through the priesthood, is the one infallible guide." —Wylie, b. 3, ch. 2.

When after a time the excitement in Prague subsided, Huss returned to his chapel of Bethlehem, to continue with greater zeal and courage the preaching of the word of God. His enemies were active and powerful, but the queen and many of the nobles were his friends, and the people in great numbers sided with him. Comparing his pure and elevating teachings and holy life with the degrading dogmas which the Romanists preached, and the avarice and debauchery which they practiced, many regarded it an honor to be on his side.

Hitherto Huss had stood alone in his labors; but now Jerome, who while in England had accepted the teachings of Wycliffe, joined in the work of reform.

The two were hereafter united in their lives, and in death they were not to be divided. Brilliancy of genius, eloquence and learning—gifts that win popular favor—were possessed in a preeminent degree by Jerome; but in those qualities which constitute real strength of character, Huss was the greater. His calm judgment served as a restraint upon the impulsive spirit of Jerome, who, with true humility, perceived his worth, and yielded to his counsels. Under their united labors the reform was more rapidly extended.

God permitted great light to shine upon the minds of these chosen men, revealing to them many of the errors of Rome; but they did not receive all the light that was to be given to the world. Through these, His servants, God was leading the people out of the darkness of Romanism; but there were many and great obstacles for them to meet, and He led them on, step by step, as they could bear it. They were not prepared to receive all the light at once. Like the full glory of the noontide sun to those who have long dwelt in darkness, it would, if presented, have caused them to turn away. Therefore He revealed it to the leaders little by little, as it could be received by the people. From century to century, other faithful workers were to follow, to lead the people on still further in the path of reform.

The schism in the church still continued. Three popes were now contending for the supremacy, and their strife filled Christendom with crime and tumult. Not content with hurling anathemas, they resorted to temporal weapons. Each cast about him to purchase arms and to obtain soldiers. Of course money must be had; and to procure this, the gifts, offices, and blessings of the church were offered for sale. The priests also, imitating their superiors, resorted to simony and war to humble their rivals and strengthen their own power. With daily increasing boldness Huss thundered against the abominations which were tolerated in the name of religion; and the people openly accused the Romish leaders as the cause of the miseries that overwhelmed Christendom.

Again the city of Prague seemed on the verge of a bloody conflict. As in former ages, God's servant was accused as "he that troubleth Israel." 1 Kings 18:17. The city was again placed under interdict, and Huss withdrew to his native village. The testimony so faithfully borne from his loved chapel of Bethlehem was ended. He was to speak from a wider stage, to all Christendom, before laying down his life as a witness for the truth.

To cure the evils that were distracting Europe, a general council was summoned to meet at Constance. The council was called at the desire of the emperor Sigismund, by one of the three rival popes, John XXIII. The demand for a council had been far from welcome to Pope John, whose character and policy could ill bear investigation, even by prelates as lax in morals as were the churchmen of those times. He dared not, however, oppose the will of Sigismund.

The chief objects to be accomplished by the council were to heal the schism in the church and to root out heresy. Hence the two antipopes were summoned to appear before it, as well as the leading propagator of the new opinions, John Huss. The former, having regard to their own safety, did not attend in person, but were represented by their delegates. Pope John, while ostensibly the convoker of the council, came to it with many misgivings, suspecting the emperor's secret purpose to depose him, and fearing to be brought to account for the vices which had disgraced the tiara, as well as for the crimes which had secured it. Yet he made his entry into the city of Constance with great pomp, attended by ecclesiastics of the highest rank and followed by a train of courtiers. All the clergy and dignitaries of the city, with an immense crowd of citizens, went out to welcome him. Above his head was a golden canopy, borne by four of the chief magistrates. The host was carried before him, and the rich dresses of the cardinals and nobles made an imposing display.

Meanwhile another traveler was approaching Constance. Huss was conscious of the dangers which threatened him. He parted from his friends as if he were never to meet them again, and went on his journey feeling that it was leading him to the stake. Notwithstanding he had obtained a safe-conduct from the king of Bohemia, and received one also from the emperor Sigismund while on his journey, he made all his arrangements in view of the probability of his death.

In a letter addressed to his friends at Prague he said: "My brethren, … I am departing with a safe-conduct from the king to meet my numerous and mortal enemies. … I confide altogether in the all-powerful God, in my Saviour; I trust that He will listen to your ardent prayers, that He will infuse His prudence and His wisdom into my mouth, in order that I may resist them; and that He will accord me His Holy Spirit to fortify me in His truth, so that I may face with courage, temptations, prison, and, if necessary, a cruel death. Jesus Christ suffered for His well-beloved; and therefore ought we to be astonished that He has left us His example, in order that we may ourselves endure with patience all things for our own salvation? He is God, and we are His creatures; He is the Lord, and we are His servants; He is Master of the world, and we are contemptible mortals—yet He suffered! Why, then, should we not suffer also, particularly when suffering is for us a purification? Therefore, beloved, if my death ought to contribute to His glory, pray that it may come quickly, and that He may enable me to support all my calamities with constancy. But if it be better that I return amongst you, let us pray to God that I may return without stain—that is, that I may not suppress one tittle of the truth of the gospel, in order to leave my brethren an excellent example to follow. Probably, therefore, you will nevermore behold my face at Prague; but should the will of the all-powerful God deign to restore me to you, let us then advance with a firmer heart in the knowledge and the love of His law." —Bonnechose, vol. 1, pp. 147, 148.

In another letter, to a priest who had become a disciple of the gospel, Huss spoke with deep humility of his own errors, accusing himself "of having felt

pleasure in wearing rich apparel and of having wasted hours in frivolous oc-
cupations." He then added these touching admonitions: "May the glory of God
and the salvation of souls occupy thy mind, and not the possession of benefices
and estates. Beware of adorning thy house more than thy soul; and, above all,
give thy care to the spiritual edifice. Be pious and humble with the poor, and
consume not thy substance in feasting. Shouldst thou not amend thy life and
refrain from superfluities, I fear that thou wilt be severely chastened, as I am
myself. ... Thou knowest my doctrine, for thou hast received my instructions
from thy childhood; it is therefore useless for me to write to thee any further.
But I conjure thee, by the mercy of our Lord, not to imitate me in any of the
vanities into which thou hast seen me fall." On the cover of the letter he added:
"I conjure thee, my friend, not to break this seal until thou shalt have acquired
the certitude that I am dead." —*Ibid.*, vol. 1, pp. 148, 149.

On his journey, Huss everywhere beheld indications of the spread of
his doctrines and the favor with which his cause was regarded. The people
thronged to meet him, and in some towns the magistrates attended him through
their streets.

Upon arriving at Constance, Huss was granted full liberty. To the emperor's
safe-conduct was added a personal assurance of protection by the pope. But, in
violation of these solemn and repeated declarations, the Reformer was in a short
time arrested, by order of the pope and cardinals, and thrust into a loathsome
dungeon. Later he was transferred to a strong castle across the Rhine and there
kept a prisoner. The pope, profiting little by his perfidy, was soon after committed
to the same prison. *Ibid.*, vol. 1, p. 247. He had been proved before the council
to be guilty of the basest crimes, besides murder, simony, and adultery, "sins
not fit to be named." So the council itself declared, and he was finally deprived
of the tiara and thrown into prison. The antipopes also were deposed, and a
new pontiff was chosen.

Though the pope himself had been guilty of greater crimes than Huss had
ever charged upon the priests, and for which he had demanded a reformation, yet the same council which degraded the pontiff proceeded to crush the
Reformer. The imprisonment of Huss excited great indignation in Bohemia.
Powerful noblemen addressed to the council earnest protests against this out-
rage. The emperor, who was loath to permit the violation of a safe-conduct,
opposed the proceedings against him. But the enemies of the Reformer were
malignant and determined. They appealed to the emperor's prejudices, to his
fears, to his zeal for the church. They brought forward arguments of great length
to prove that "faith ought not to be kept with heretics, nor persons suspected
of heresy, though they are furnished with safe-conducts from the emperor and
kings." —Jacques Lenfant, *History of the Council of Constance*, vol. 1, p. 516.
Thus they prevailed.

Enfeebled by illness and imprisonment,—for the damp, foul air of his dungeon had brought on a fever which nearly ended his life,—Huss was at last brought before the council. Loaded with chains he stood in the presence of the emperor, whose honor and good faith had been pledged to protect him. During his long trial he firmly maintained the truth, and in the presence of the assembled dignitaries of church and state he uttered a solemn and faithful protest against the corruptions of the hierarchy. When required to choose whether he would recant his doctrines or suffer death, he accepted the martyr's fate.

The grace of God sustained him. During the weeks of suffering that passed before his final sentence, heaven's peace filled his soul. "I write this letter," he said to a friend, "in my prison, and with my fettered hand, expecting my sentence of death tomorrow. … When, with the assistance of Jesus Christ, we shall again meet in the delicious peace of the future life, you will learn how merciful God has shown Himself toward me, how effectually He has supported me in the midst of my temptations and trials." —Bonnechose, vol. 2, p. 67.

In the gloom of his dungeon he foresaw the triumph of the true faith. Returning in his dreams to the chapel at Prague where he had preached the gospel, he saw the pope and his bishops effacing the pictures of Christ which he had painted on its walls. "This vision distressed him: but on the next day he saw many painters occupied in restoring these figures in greater number and in brighter colors. As soon as their task was ended, the painters, who were surrounded by an immense crowd, exclaimed, 'Now let the popes and bishops come; they shall never efface them more!'" Said the Reformer, as he related his dream: "I maintain this for certain, that the image of Christ will never be effaced. They have wished to destroy it, but it shall be painted afresh in all hearts by much better preachers than myself." —D'Aubigne, b. 1, ch. 6.

For the last time, Huss was brought before the council. It was a vast and brilliant assembly—the emperor, the princes of the empire, the royal deputies, the cardinals, bishops, and priests, and an immense crowd who had come as spectators of the events of the day. From all parts of Christendom had been gathered the witnesses of this first great sacrifice in the long struggle by which liberty of conscience was to be secured.

Being called upon for his final decision, Huss declared his refusal to abjure, and, fixing his penetrating glance upon the monarch whose plighted word had been so shamelessly violated, he declared: "I determined, of my own free will, to appear before this council, under the public protection and faith of the emperor here present." —Bonnechose, vol. 2, p. 84. A deep flush crimsoned the face of Sigismund as the eyes of all in the assembly turned upon him.

Sentence having been pronounced, the ceremony of degradation began. The bishops clothed their prisoner in the sacerdotal habit, and as he took the priestly robe, he said: "Our Lord Jesus Christ was covered with a white robe, by way of insult, when Herod had Him conducted before Pilate." —*Ibid.*, vol. 2, p. 86. Being again exhorted to retract, he replied, turning toward the people: "With what face, then, should I behold the heavens? How should I look on those multitudes of men to whom I have preached the pure gospel? No; I esteem their salvation more than this poor body, now appointed unto death." The vestments were removed one by one, each bishop pronouncing a curse as he performed his part of the ceremony. Finally "they put on his head a cap or pyramidal-shaped miter of paper, on which were painted frightful figures of demons, with the word 'Archheretic' conspicuous in front. 'Most joyfully,' said Huss, 'will I wear this crown of shame for Thy sake, O Jesus, who for me didst wear a crown of thorns.'"

When he was thus arrayed, "the prelates said, 'Now we devote thy soul to the devil.' 'And I,' said John Huss, lifting up his eyes toward heaven, 'do commit my spirit into Thy hands, O Lord Jesus, for Thou hast redeemed me.'" —Wylie, b. 3, ch. 7.

He was now delivered up to the secular authorities and led away to the place of execution. An immense procession followed, hundreds of men at arms, priests and bishops in their costly robes, and the inhabitants of Constance. When he had been fastened to the stake, and all was ready for the fire to be lighted, the martyr was once more exhorted to save himself by renouncing his errors. "What errors," said Huss, "shall I renounce? I know myself guilty of none. I call God to witness that all that I have written and preached has been with the view of rescuing souls from sin and perdition; and, therefore, most joyfully will I confirm with my blood that truth which I have written and preached." —*Ibid.*, b. 3, ch. 7. When the flames kindled about him, he began to sing, "Jesus, Thou Son of David, have mercy on me," and so continued till his voice was silenced forever.

Even his enemies were struck with his heroic bearing. A zealous papist, describing the martyrdom of Huss, and of Jerome, who died soon after, said: "Both bore themselves with constant mind when their last hour approached. They prepared for the fire as if they were going to a marriage feast. They uttered no cry of pain. When the flames rose, they began to sing hymns; and scarce could the vehemency of the fire stop their singing." —*Ibid.*, b. 3, ch. 7.

When the body of Huss had been wholly consumed, his ashes, with the soil upon which they rested, were gathered up and cast into the Rhine, and thus borne onward to the ocean. His persecutors vainly imagined that they had rooted out the truths he preached. Little did they dream that the ashes that day borne away to the sea were to be as seed scattered in all the countries of the earth; that in lands yet unknown it would yield abundant fruit in witnesses for the truth. The voice which had spoken in the council hall of Constance had wakened echoes that would be heard through all coming ages. Huss was no more, but the truths for which he died could never perish. His example of faith and constancy would encourage multitudes to stand firm for the truth, in the face of torture and death. His execution had exhibited to the whole world the perfidious cruelty of Rome. The enemies of truth, though they knew it not, had been furthering the cause which they vainly sought to destroy.

Yet another stake was to be set up at Constance. The blood of another witness must testify for the truth. Jerome, upon bidding farewell to Huss on his departure for the council, had exhorted him to courage and firmness, declaring that if he should fall into any peril, he himself would fly to his assistance. Upon hearing of the Reformer's imprisonment, the faithful disciple immediately prepared to fulfill his promise. Without a safe-conduct he set out, with a single companion, for Constance. On arriving there he was convinced that he had only exposed himself to peril, without the possibility of doing anything for the deliverance of Huss. He fled from the city, but was arrested on the homeward journey and brought back loaded with fetters and under the custody of a band of soldiers. At his first appearance before the council his attempts to reply to the accusations brought against him were met with shouts, "To the flames with him! to the flames!" —Bonnechose, vol. 1, p. 234. He was thrown into a dungeon, chained in a position which caused him great suffering, and fed on bread and water. After some months the cruelties of his imprisonment brought upon Jerome an illness that threatened his life, and his enemies, fearing that he might escape them, treated him with less severity, though he remained in prison for one year.

The death of Huss had not resulted as the papists had hoped. The violation of his safe-conduct had roused a storm of indignation, and as the safer course, the council determined, instead of burning Jerome, to force him, if possible, to retract. He was brought before the assembly, and offered the alternative to recant, or to die at the stake. Death at the beginning of his imprisonment would have been a mercy in comparison with the terrible sufferings which he had undergone; but now, weakened by illness, by the rigors of his prison house, and the torture of anxiety and suspense, separated from his friends, and disheartened by the death of Huss, Jerome's fortitude gave way, and he consented to submit to the council. He pledged himself to adhere to the Catholic faith, and accepted the action of the council in condemning the doctrines of Wycliffe and Huss, excepting, however, the "holy truths" which they had taught. —*Ibid*, vol. 2, p. 141.

By this expedient Jerome endeavored to silence the voice of conscience and escape his doom. But in the solitude of his dungeon he saw more clearly what he had done. He thought of the courage and fidelity of Huss, and in contrast pondered upon his own denial of the truth. He thought of the divine Master whom he had pledged himself to serve, and who for his sake endured the death of the cross. Before his retraction he had found comfort, amid all his sufferings, in the assurance of God's favor; but now remorse and doubts tortured his soul. He knew that still other retractions must be made before he could be at peace with Rome. The path upon which he was entering could end only in complete apostasy. His resolution was taken: To escape a brief period of suffering he would not deny his Lord.

Soon he was again brought before the council. His submission had not satisfied his judges. Their thirst for blood, whetted by the death of Huss, clamored for fresh victims. Only by an unreserved surrender of the truth could Jerome preserve his life. But he had determined to avow his faith and follow his brother martyr to the flames.

He renounced his former recantation and, as a dying man, solemnly required an opportunity to make his defense. Fearing the effect of his words, the prelates insisted that he should merely affirm or deny the truth of the charges brought against him. Jerome protested against such cruelty and injustice. "You have held me shut up three hundred and forty days in a frightful prison," he said, "in the midst of filth, noisomeness, stench, and the utmost want of everything; you then bring me out before you, and lending an ear to my mortal enemies, you refuse to hear me. ... If you be really wise men, and the lights of the world, take care not to sin against justice. As to me, I am only a feeble mortal; my life is but of little importance; and when I exhort you not to deliver an unjust sentence, I speak less for myself than for you." —*Ibid.*, vol. 2, pp. 146, 147.

His request was finally granted. In the presence of his judges, Jerome kneeled down and prayed that the divine Spirit might control his thoughts and words, that he might speak nothing contrary to the truth or unworthy of his Master. To him that day was fulfilled the promise of God to the first disciples: "Ye shall be brought before governors and kings for My sake. ... But when they deliver you up, take no thought how or what ye shall speak: for it shall be given you in that same hour what ye shall speak. For it is not ye that speak, but the Spirit of your Father which speaketh in you." Matthew 10:18-20.

The words of Jerome excited astonishment and admiration, even in his enemies. For a whole year he had been immured in a dungeon, unable to read or even to see, in great physical suffering and mental anxiety. Yet his arguments were presented with as much clearness and power as if he had had undisturbed opportunity for study. He pointed his hearers to the long line of holy men who had been condemned by unjust judges. In almost every generation have been those who, while seeking to elevate the people of their time, have been reproached and cast out, but who in later times have been shown to be deserving of honor. Christ Himself was condemned as a malefactor at an unrighteous tribunal.

At his retraction, Jerome had assented to the justice of the sentence condemning Huss; he now declared his repentance and bore witness to the innocence and holiness of the martyr. "I knew him from his childhood," he said. "He was a most excellent man, just and holy; he was condemned, notwithstanding his innocence. ... I also—I am ready to die: I will not recoil before the torments that are prepared for me by my enemies and false witnesses, who will one day have to render an account of their impostures before the great God, whom nothing can deceive." —Bonnechose, vol. 2, p. 151.

In self-reproach for his own denial of the truth, Jerome continued: "Of all the sins that I have committed since my youth, none weigh so heavily on my mind, and cause me such poignant remorse, as that which I committed in this fatal place, when I approved of the iniquitous sentence rendered against Wycliffe, and against the holy martyr, John Huss, my master and my friend. Yes! I confess it from my heart, and declare with horror that I disgracefully quailed when, through a dread of death, I condemned their doctrines. I therefore supplicate ... Almighty God to deign to pardon me my sins, and this one in particular, the most heinous of all." Pointing to his judges, he said firmly: "You condemned Wycliffe and John Huss, not for having shaken the doctrine of the church, but simply because they branded with reprobation the scandals proceeding from the clergy—their pomp, their pride, and all the vices of the prelates and priests. The things which they have affirmed, and which are irrefutable, I also think and declare, like them."

His words were interrupted. The prelates, trembling with rage, cried out: "What need is there of further proof? We behold with our own eyes the most obstinate of heretics!"

Unmoved by the tempest, Jerome exclaimed: "What! do you suppose that I fear to die? You have held me for a whole year in a frightful dungeon, more horrible than death itself. You have treated me more cruelly than a Turk, Jew, or pagan, and my flesh has literally rotted off my bones alive; and yet I make no complaint, for lamentation ill becomes a man of heart and spirit; but I cannot but express my astonishment at such great barbarity toward a Christian." —*Ibid.*, vol. 2, pp. 151-153.

Again the storm of rage burst out, and Jerome was hurried away to prison. Yet there were some in the assembly upon whom his words had made a deep impression and who desired to save his life. He was visited by dignitaries of the church and urged to submit himself to the council. The most brilliant prospects were presented before him as the reward of renouncing his opposition to Rome. But like his Master when offered the glory of the world, Jerome remained steadfast.

"Prove to me from the Holy Writings that I am in error," he said, "and I will abjure it."

"The Holy Writings!" exclaimed one of his tempters, "is everything then to be judged by them? Who can understand them till the church has interpreted them?"

"Are the traditions of men more worthy of faith than the gospel of our Saviour?" replied Jerome. "Paul did not exhort those to whom he wrote to listen to the traditions of men, but said, 'Search the Scriptures.'"

"Heretic!" was the response, "I repent having pleaded so long with you. I see that you are urged on by the devil." —Wylie, b. 3, ch. 10.

Erelong sentence of condemnation was passed upon him. He was led out to the same spot upon which Huss had yielded up his life. He went singing on his way, his countenance lighted up with joy and peace. His gaze was fixed upon Christ, and to him death had lost its terrors. When the executioner, about to kindle the pile, stepped behind him, the martyr exclaimed: "Come forward boldly; apply the fire before my face. Had I been afraid, I should not be here."

His last words, uttered as the flames rose about him, were a prayer. "Lord, Almighty Father," he cried, "have pity on me, and pardon me my sins; for Thou knowest that I have always loved Thy truth." —Bonnechose, vol. 2, p. 168. His voice ceased, but his lips continued to move in prayer. When the fire had done its work, the ashes of the martyr, with the earth upon which they rested, were gathered up, and like those of Huss, were thrown into the Rhine.

So perished God's faithful light bearers. But the light of the truths which they proclaimed—the light of their heroic example—could not be extinguished. As well might men attempt to turn back the sun in its course as to prevent the dawning of that day which was even then breaking upon the world.

The execution of Huss had kindled a flame of indignation and horror in Bohemia. It was felt by the whole nation that he had fallen a prey to the malice of the priests and the treachery of the emperor. He was declared to have been a faithful teacher of the truth, and the council that decreed his death was charged with the guilt of murder. His doctrines now attracted greater attention than ever before. By the papal edicts the writings of Wycliffe had been condemned to the flames. But those that had escaped destruction were now brought out from their hiding places and studied in connection with the Bible, or such parts of it as the people could obtain, and many were thus led to accept the reformed faith.

The murderers of Huss did not stand quietly by and witness the triumph of his cause. The pope and the emperor united to crush out the movement, and the armies of Sigismund were hurled upon Bohemia.

But a deliverer was raised up. Ziska, who soon after the opening of the war became totally blind, yet who was one of the ablest generals of his age, was the leader of the Bohemians. Trusting in the help of God and the righteousness of their cause, that people withstood the mightiest armies that could be brought against them. Again and again the emperor, raising fresh armies, invaded Bohemia, only to be ignominiously repulsed. The Hussites were raised above the fear of death, and nothing could stand against them. A few years after the opening of the war, the brave Ziska died; but his place was filled by Procopius, who was an equally brave and skillful general, and in some respects a more able leader.

The enemies of the Bohemians, knowing that the blind warrior was dead, deemed the opportunity favorable for recovering all that they had lost. The pope now proclaimed a crusade against the Hussites, and again an immense force was precipitated upon Bohemia, but only to suffer terrible defeat. Another crusade was proclaimed. In all the papal countries of Europe, men, money, and munitions of war were raised. Multitudes flocked to the papal standard, assured that at last an end would be made of the Hussite heretics. Confident of victory, the vast force entered Bohemia. The people rallied to repel them. The two armies approached each other until only a river lay between them. "The crusaders were in greatly superior force, but instead of dashing across the stream, and closing in battle with the Hussites whom they had come so far to meet, they stood gazing in silence at those warriors." —Wylie, b. 3, ch. 17. Then suddenly a mysterious terror fell upon the host. Without striking a blow, that mighty force broke and scattered as if dispelled by an unseen power. Great numbers were slaughtered by the Hussite army, which pursued the fugitives, and an immense booty fell into the hands of the victors, so that the war, instead of impoverishing, enriched the Bohemians.

A few years later, under a new pope, still another crusade was set on foot. As before, men and means were drawn from all the papal countries of Europe. Great were the inducements held out to those who should engage in this perilous enterprise. Full forgiveness of the most heinous crimes was ensured to every crusader. All who died in the war were promised a rich reward in heaven, and those who survived were to reap honor and riches on the field of battle. Again a vast army was collected, and, crossing the frontier they entered Bohemia. The Hussite forces fell back before them, thus drawing the invaders farther and farther into the country, and leading them to count the victory already won. At last the army of Procopius made a stand, and turning upon the foe, advanced to give them battle. The crusaders, now discovering their mistake, lay in their encampment awaiting the onset. As the sound of the approaching force was heard, even before the Hussites were in sight, a panic again fell upon the crusaders. Princes, generals, and common soldiers, casting away their armor, fled in all directions. In vain the papal legate, who was the leader of the invasion, endeavored to rally his terrified and disorganized forces. Despite his utmost endeavors, he himself was swept along in the tide of fugitives. The rout was complete, and again an immense booty fell into the hands of the victors.

Thus the second time a vast army, sent forth by the most powerful nations of Europe, a host of brave, warlike men, trained and equipped for battle, fled without a blow before the defenders of a small and hitherto feeble nation. Here was a manifestation of divine power. The invaders were smitten with a supernatural terror. He who overthrew the hosts of Pharaoh in the Red Sea, who put to flight the armies of Midian before Gideon and his three hundred, who in one night laid low the forces of the proud Assyrian, had again stretched out His hand to wither the power of the oppressor. "There were they in great fear, where no fear was: for God hath scattered the bones of him that encampeth against thee: thou hast put them to shame, because God hath despised them." Psalm 53:5.

The papal leaders, despairing of conquering by force, at last resorted to diplomacy. A compromise was entered into, that while professing to grant to the Bohemians freedom of conscience, really betrayed them into the power of Rome. The Bohemians had specified four points as the condition of peace with Rome: the free preaching of the Bible; the right of the whole church to both the bread and the wine in the communion, and the use of the mother tongue in divine worship; the exclusion of the clergy from all secular offices and authority; and, in cases of crime, the jurisdiction of the civil courts over clergy and laity alike. The papal authorities at last "agreed that the four articles of the Hussites should be accepted, but that the right of explaining them, that is, of determining their precise import, should belong to the council—in other words, to the pope and the emperor." —Wylie, b. 3, ch. 18. On this basis a treaty was entered into, and Rome gained by dissimulation and fraud what she had failed to gain by conflict; for, placing her own interpretation upon the Hussite articles, as upon the Bible, she could pervert their meaning to suit her own purposes.

A large class in Bohemia, seeing that it betrayed their liberties, could not consent to the compact. Dissensions and divisions arose, leading to strife and bloodshed among themselves. In this strife the noble Procopius fell, and the liberties of Bohemia perished.

Sigismund, the betrayer of Huss and Jerome, now became king of Bohemia, and regardless of his oath to support the rights of the Bohemians, he proceeded to establish popery. But he had gained little by his subservience to Rome. For twenty years his life had been filled with labors and perils. His armies had been wasted and his treasuries drained by a long and fruitless struggle; and now, after reigning one year, he died, leaving his kingdom on the brink of civil war, and bequeathing to posterity a name branded with infamy.

Tumults, strife, and bloodshed were protracted. Again foreign armies invaded Bohemia, and internal dissension continued to distract the nation. Those who remained faithful to the gospel were subjected to a bloody persecution.

As their former brethren, entering into compact with Rome, imbibed her errors, those who adhered to the ancient faith had formed themselves into a distinct church, taking the name of "United Brethren." This act drew upon them maledictions from all classes. Yet their firmness was unshaken. Forced to find refuge in the woods and caves, they still assembled to read God's word and unite in His worship.

Through messengers secretly sent out into different countries, they learned that here and there were "isolated confessors of the truth, a few in this city and a few in that, the object, like themselves, of persecution; and that amid the mountains of the Alps was an ancient church, resting on the foundations of Scripture, and protesting against the idolatrous corruptions of Rome." —Wylie, b. 3, ch. 19. This intelligence was received with great joy, and a correspondence was opened with the Waldensian Christians.

Steadfast to the gospel, the Bohemians waited through the night of their persecution, in the darkest hour still turning their eyes toward the horizon like men who watch for the morning. "Their lot was cast in evil days, but … they remembered the words first uttered by Huss, and repeated by Jerome, that a century must revolve before the day should break. These were to the Taborites [Hussites] what the words of Joseph were to the tribes in the house of bondage: 'I die, and God will surely visit you, and bring you out.'" —*Ibid.*, b. 3, ch. 19. "The closing period of the fifteenth century witnessed the slow but sure increase of the churches of the Brethren. Although far from being unmolested, they yet enjoyed comparative rest. At the commencement of the sixteenth century their churches numbered two hundred in Bohemia and Moravia." —Ezra Hall Gillett, *Life and Times of John Huss*, vol. 2, p. 570. "So goodly was the remnant which, escaping the destructive fury of fire and sword, was permitted to see the dawning of that day which Huss had foretold." —Wylie, b. 3, ch. 19.

Four

—Luther's Separation From Rome—

Foremost among those who were called to lead the church from the darkness of popery into the light of a purer faith, stood Martin Luther. Zealous, ardent, and devoted, knowing no fear but the fear of God, and acknowledging no foundation for religious faith but the Holy Scriptures, Luther was the man for his time; through him God accomplished a great work for the reformation of the church and the enlightenment of the world.

Like the first heralds of the gospel, Luther sprang from the ranks of poverty. His early years were spent in the humble home of a German peasant. By daily toil as a miner his father earned the means for his education. He intended him for a lawyer; but God purposed to make him a builder in the great temple that was rising so slowly through the centuries. Hardship, privation, and severe discipline were the school in which Infinite Wisdom prepared Luther for the important mission of his life.

Luther's father was a man of strong and active mind and great force of character, honest, resolute, and straightforward. He was true to his convictions of duty, let the consequences be what they might. His sterling good sense led him to regard the monastic system with distrust. He was highly displeased when Luther, without his consent, entered a monastery; and it was two years before the father was reconciled to his son, and even then his opinions remained the same.

Luther's parents bestowed great care upon the education and training of their children. They endeavored to instruct them in the knowledge of God and the practice of Christian virtues. The father's prayer often ascended in the hearing of his son that the child might remember the name of the Lord and one day aid in the advancement of His truth. Every advantage for moral or intellectual culture which their life of toil permitted them to enjoy was eagerly improved by these parents. Their efforts were earnest and persevering to prepare their children for a life of piety and usefulness. With their firmness and strength of character they sometimes exercised too great severity; but the Reformer himself, though conscious that in some respects they had erred, found in their discipline more to approve than to condemn.

At school, where he was sent at an early age, Luther was treated with harshness and even violence. So great was the poverty of his parents that upon going from home to school in another town he was for a time obliged to obtain his food by singing from door to door, and he often suffered from hunger. The gloomy, superstitious ideas of religion then prevailing filled him with fear. He would lie down at night with a sorrowful heart, looking forward with trembling to the dark future and in constant terror at the thought of God as a stern, unrelenting judge, a cruel tyrant, rather than a kind heavenly Father.

Yet under so many and so great discouragements Luther pressed resolutely forward toward the high standard of moral and intellectual excellence which attracted his soul. He thirsted for knowledge, and the earnest and practical character of his mind led him to desire the solid and useful rather than the showy and superficial.

When, at the age of eighteen, he entered the University of Erfurt, his situation was more favorable and his prospects were brighter than in his earlier years. His parents having by thrift and industry acquired a competence, they were able to render him all needed assistance. And the influence of judicious friends had somewhat lessened the gloomy effects of his former training. He applied himself to the study of the best authors, diligently treasuring their most weighty thoughts and making the wisdom of the wise his own. Even under the harsh discipline of his former instructors he had early given promise of distinction, and with favorable influences his mind rapidly developed. A retentive memory, a lively imagination, strong reasoning powers, and untiring application soon placed him in the foremost rank among his associates. Intellectual discipline ripened his understanding and aroused an activity of mind and a keenness of perception that were preparing him for the conflicts of his life.

The fear of the Lord dwelt in the heart of Luther, enabling him to maintain his steadfastness of purpose and leading him to deep humility before God. He had an abiding sense of his dependence upon divine aid, and he did not fail to begin each day with prayer, while his heart was continually breathing a petition for guidance and support. "To pray well," he often said, "is the better half of study." —D'Aubigne, b. 2, ch. 2.

While one day examining the books in the library of the university, Luther discovered a Latin Bible. Such a book he had never before seen. He was ignorant even of its existence. He had heard portions of the Gospels and Epistles, which were read to the people at public worship, and he supposed that these were the entire Bible. Now, for the first time, he looked upon the whole of God's word. With mingled awe and wonder he turned the sacred pages; with quickened pulse and throbbing heart he read for himself the words of life, pausing now and then to exclaim: "O that God would give me such a book for myself!" —*Ibid.*, b. 2, ch. 2. Angels of heaven were by his side, and rays of light from the throne of God revealed the treasures of truth to his understanding. He had ever feared to offend God, but now the deep conviction of his condition as a sinner took hold upon him as never before.

An earnest desire to be free from sin and to find peace with God led him at last to enter a cloister and devote himself to a monastic life. Here he was required to perform the lowest drudgery and to beg from house to house. He was at an age when respect and appreciation are most eagerly craved, and these menial offices were deeply mortifying to his natural feelings; but he patiently endured this humiliation, believing that it was necessary because of his sins.

Every moment that could be spared from his daily duties he employed in study, robbing himself of sleep and grudging even the time spent at his scanty meals. Above everything else he delighted in the study of God's word. He had found a Bible chained to the convent wall, and to this he often repaired. As his convictions of sin deepened, he sought by his own works to obtain pardon and peace. He led a most rigorous life, endeavoring by fasting, vigils, and scourgings to subdue the evils of his nature, from which the monastic life had brought no release. He shrank from no sacrifice by which he might attain to that purity of heart which would enable him to stand approved before God. "I was indeed a pious monk," he afterward said, "and followed the rules of my order more strictly than I can express. If ever monk could obtain heaven by his monkish works, I should certainly have been entitled to it. ... If it had continued much longer, I should have carried my mortifications even to death." —*Ibid.*, b. 2, ch. 3. As the result of this painful discipline he lost strength and suffered from fainting spasms, from the effects of which he never fully recovered. But with all his efforts his burdened soul found no relief. He was at last driven to the verge of despair.

When it appeared to Luther that all was lost, God raised up a friend and helper for him. The pious Staupitz opened the word of God to Luther's mind and bade him look away from himself, cease the contemplation of infinite punishment for the violation of God's law, and look to Jesus, his sin-pardoning Saviour. "Instead of torturing yourself on account of your sins, throw yourself into the Redeemer's arms. Trust in Him, in the righteousness of His life, in the atonement of His death. ... Listen to the Son of God. He became man to give you the assurance of divine favor." "Love Him who first loved you." —*Ibid.*, b. 2, ch. 4. Thus spoke this messenger of mercy. His words made a deep impression upon Luther's mind. After many a struggle with long-cherished errors, he was enabled to grasp the truth, and peace came to his troubled soul.

Luther was ordained a priest and was called from the cloister to a professorship in the University of Wittenberg. Here he applied himself to the study of the Scriptures in the original tongues. He began to lecture upon the Bible; and the book of Psalms, the Gospels, and the Epistles were opened to the understanding of crowds of delighted listeners. Staupitz, his friend and superior, urged him to ascend the pulpit and preach the word of God. Luther hesitated, feeling himself unworthy to speak to the people in Christ's stead. It was only after a long struggle that he yielded to the solicitations of his friends. Already he was mighty in the Scriptures, and the grace of God rested upon him. His eloquence captivated his hearers, the clearness and power with which he presented the truth convinced their understanding, and his fervor touched their hearts.

Luther was still a true son of the papal church and had no thought that he would ever be anything else. In the providence of God he was led to visit Rome. He pursued his journey on foot, lodging at the monasteries on the way. At a convent in Italy he was filled with wonder at the wealth, magnificence, and luxury that he witnessed. Endowed with a princely revenue, the monks dwelt in splendid apartments, attired themselves in the richest and most costly robes, and feasted at a sumptuous table. With painful misgivings Luther contrasted this scene with the self-denial and hardship of his own life. His mind was becoming perplexed.

At last he beheld in the distance the seven-hilled city. With deep emotion he prostrated himself upon the earth, exclaiming: "Holy Rome, I salute thee!" —*Ibid.*, b. 2, ch. 6. He entered the city, visited the churches, listened to the marvelous tales repeated by priests and monks, and performed all the ceremonies required. Everywhere he looked upon scenes that filled him with astonishment and horror. He saw that iniquity existed among all classes of the clergy. He heard indecent jokes from prelates, and was filled with horror at their awful profanity, even during mass. As he mingled with the monks and citizens he met dissipation, debauchery. Turn where he would, in the place of sanctity he found profanation. "No one can imagine," he wrote, "what sins and infamous actions are committed in Rome; they must be seen and heard to be believed. Thus they are in the habit of saying, 'If there is a hell, Rome is built over it: it is an abyss whence issues every kind of sin.'" —*Ibid.*, b. 2, ch. 6.

By a recent decretal an indulgence had been promised by the pope to all who should ascend upon their knees "Pilate's staircase," said to have been descended by our Saviour on leaving the Roman judgment hall and to have been miraculously conveyed from Jerusalem to Rome. Luther was one day devoutly climbing these steps, when suddenly a voice like thunder seemed to say to him: "The just shall live by faith." Romans 1:17. He sprang to his feet and hastened from the place in shame and horror. That text never lost its power upon his soul. From that time he saw more clearly than ever before the fallacy of trusting to human works for salvation, and the necessity of constant faith in the merits of Christ. His eyes had been opened, and were never again to be closed, to the delusions of the papacy. When he turned his face from Rome he had turned away also in heart, and from that time the separation grew wider, until he severed all connection with the papal church.

After his return from Rome, Luther received at the University of Wittenberg the degree of doctor of divinity. Now he was at liberty to devote himself, as never before, to the Scriptures that he loved. He had taken a solemn vow to study carefully and to preach with fidelity the word of God, not the sayings and doctrines of the popes, all the days of his life. He was no longer the mere monk or professor, but the authorized herald of the Bible. He had been called as a shepherd to feed the flock of God, that were hungering and thirsting for the truth. He firmly declared that Christians should receive no other doctrines than those which rest on the authority of the Sacred Scriptures. These words struck at the very foundation of papal supremacy. They contained the vital principle of the Reformation.

Luther saw the danger of exalting human theories above the word of God. He fearlessly attacked the speculative infidelity of the schoolmen and opposed the philosophy and theology which had so long held a controlling influence upon the people. He denounced such studies as not only worthless but pernicious, and sought to turn the minds of his hearers from the sophistries of philosophers and theologians to the eternal truths set forth by prophets and apostles.

Precious was the message which he bore to the eager crowds that hung upon his words. Never before had such teachings fallen upon their ears. The glad tidings of a Saviour's love, the assurance of pardon and peace through His atoning blood, rejoiced their hearts and inspired within them an immortal hope. At Wittenberg a light was kindled whose rays should extend to the uttermost parts of the earth, and which was to increase in brightness to the close of time.

But light and darkness cannot harmonize. Between truth and error there is an irrepressible conflict. To uphold and defend the one is to attack and overthrow the other. Our Saviour Himself declared: "I came not to send peace, but a sword." Matthew 10:34. Said Luther, a few years after the opening of the Reformation: "God does not guide me, He pushes me forward. He carries me away. I am not master of myself. I desire to live in repose; but I am thrown into the midst of tumults and revolutions." —D'Aubigne, b. 5, ch. 2. He was now about to be urged into the contest.

The Roman Church had made merchandise of the grace of God. The tables of the money-changers (Matthew 21:12) were set up beside her altars, and the air resounded with the shouts of buyers and sellers. Under the plea of raising funds for the erection of St. Peter's Church at Rome, indulgences for sin were publicly offered for sale by the authority of the pope. By the price of crime a temple was to be built up for God's worship—the cornerstone laid with the wages of iniquity! But the very means adopted for Rome's aggrandizement provoked the deadliest blow to her power and greatness. It was this that aroused the most determined and successful of the enemies of popery, and led to the battle which shook the papal throne and jostled the triple crown upon the pontiff's head.

The official appointed to conduct the sale of indulgences in Germany—Tetzel by name—had been convicted of the basest offenses against society and against the law of God; but having escaped the punishment due for his crimes, he was employed to further the mercenary and unscrupulous projects of the pope. With great effrontery he repeated the most glaring falsehoods and related marvelous tales to deceive an ignorant, credulous, and superstitious people. Had they possessed the word of God they would not have been thus deceived. It was to keep them under the control of the papacy, in order to swell the power and wealth of her ambitious leaders, that the Bible had been withheld from them. (See John C. L. Gieseler, *A Compendium of Ecclesiastical History*, per. 4, sec. 1, par. 5.)

As Tetzel entered a town, a messenger went before him, announcing: "The grace of God and of the holy father is at your gates." —D'Aubigne, b. 3, ch. 1. And the people welcomed the blasphemous pretender as if he were God Himself come down from heaven to them. The infamous traffic was set up in the church, and Tetzel, ascending the pulpit, extolled the indulgences as the most precious gift of God. He declared that by virtue of his certificates of pardon all the sins which the purchaser should afterward desire to commit would be forgiven him, and that "not even repentance is necessary." —*Ibid.*, b. 3, ch. 1. More than this, he assured his hearers that the indulgences had power to save not only the living but the dead; that the very moment the money should clink against the bottom of his chest, the soul in whose behalf it had been paid would escape from purgatory and make its way to heaven. (See K. R. Hagenbach, *History of the Reformation*, vol. 1, p. 96.)

When Simon Magus offered to purchase of the apostles the power to work miracles, Peter answered him: "Thy money perish with thee, because thou hast thought that the gift of God may be purchased with money." Acts 8:20. But Tetzel's offer was grasped by eager thousands. Gold and silver flowed into his treasury. A salvation that could be bought with money was more easily obtained than that which requires repentance, faith, and diligent effort to resist and overcome sin.

The doctrine of indulgences had been opposed by men of learning and piety in the Roman Church, and there were many who had no faith in pretensions so contrary to both reason and revelation. No prelate dared lift his voice against this iniquitous traffic; but the minds of men were becoming disturbed and uneasy, and many eagerly inquired if God would not work through some instrumentality for the purification of His church.

Luther, though still a papist of the straitest sort, was filled with horror at the blasphemous assumptions of the indulgence mongers. Many of his own congregation had purchased certificates of pardon, and they soon began to come to their pastor, confessing their various sins, and expecting absolution, not because they were penitent and wished to reform, but on the ground of the indulgence. Luther refused them absolution, and warned them that unless they should repent and reform their lives, they must perish in their sins. In great perplexity they repaired to Tetzel with the complaint that their confessor had refused his certificates; and some boldly demanded that their money be returned to them. The friar was filled with rage. He uttered the most terrible curses, caused fires to be lighted in the public squares, and declared that he "had received an order from the pope to burn all heretics who presumed to oppose his most holy indulgences." —D'Aubigne, b. 3, ch. 4.

Luther now entered boldly upon his work as a champion of the truth. His voice was heard from the pulpit in earnest, solemn warning. He set before the people the offensive character of sin, and taught them that it is impossible for man, by his own works, to lessen its guilt or evade its punishment. Nothing but repentance toward God and faith in Christ can save the sinner. The grace of Christ cannot be purchased; it is a free gift. He counseled the people not to buy indulgences, but to look in faith to a crucified Redeemer. He related his own painful experience in vainly seeking by humiliation and penance to secure salvation, and assured his hearers that it was by looking away from himself and believing in Christ that he found peace and joy.

As Tetzel continued his traffic and his impious pretensions, Luther determined upon a more effectual protest against these crying abuses. An occasion soon offered. The castle church of Wittenberg possessed many relics, which on certain holy days were exhibited to the people, and full remission of sins was granted to all who then visited the church and made confession. Accordingly on these days the people in great numbers resorted thither. One of the most important of these occasions, the festival of All Saints, was approaching. On the preceding day, Luther, joining the crowds that were already making their way to the church, posted on its door a paper containing ninety-five propositions against the doctrine of indulgences. He declared his willingness to defend these theses next day at the university, against all who should see fit to attack them.

His propositions attracted universal attention. They were read and reread, and repeated in every direction. Great excitement was created in the university and in the whole city. By these theses it was shown that the power to grant the pardon of sin, and to remit its penalty, had never been committed to the pope or to any other man. The whole scheme was a farce,—an artifice to extort money by playing upon the superstitions of the people,—a device of Satan to destroy the souls of all who should trust to its lying pretensions. It was also clearly shown that the gospel of Christ is the most valuable treasure of the church, and that the grace of God, therein revealed, is freely bestowed upon all who seek it by repentance and faith.

Luther's theses challenged discussion; but no one dared accept the challenge. The questions which he proposed had in a few days spread through all Germany, and in a few weeks they had sounded throughout Christendom. Many devoted Romanists, who had seen and lamented the terrible iniquity prevailing in the church, but had not known how to arrest its progress, read the propositions with great joy, recognizing in them the voice of God. They felt that the Lord had graciously set His hand to arrest the rapidly swelling tide of corruption that was issuing from the see of Rome. Princes and magistrates secretly rejoiced that a check was to be put upon the arrogant power which denied the right of appeal from its decisions.

But the sin-loving and superstitious multitudes were terrified as the sophistries that had soothed their fears were swept away. Crafty ecclesiastics, interrupted in their work of sanctioning crime, and seeing their gains endangered, were enraged, and rallied to uphold their pretensions. The Reformer had bitter accusers to meet. Some charged him with acting hastily and from impulse. Others accused him of presumption, declaring that he was not directed of God, but was acting from pride and forwardness. "Who does not know," he responded, "that a man rarely puts forth any new idea without having some appearance of pride, and without being accused of exciting quarrels? ... Why were Christ and all the martyrs put to death? Because they seemed to be proud contemners of the wisdom of the time, and because they advanced novelties without having first humbly taken counsel of the oracles of the ancient opinions."

Again he declared: "Whatever I do will be done, not by the prudence of men, but by the counsel of God. If the work be of God, who shall stop it? if it be not, who can forward it? Not my will, nor theirs, nor ours; but Thy will, O holy Father, which art in heaven." —*Ibid.*, b. 3, ch. 6.

Though Luther had been moved by the Spirit of God to begin his work, he was not to carry it forward without severe conflicts. The reproaches of his enemies, their misrepresentation of his purposes, and their unjust and malicious reflections upon his character and motives, came in upon him like an overwhelming flood; and they were not without effect. He had felt confident that the leaders of the people, both in the church and in the schools, would gladly unite with him in efforts for reform. Words of encouragement from those in high position had inspired him with joy and hope. Already in anticipation he had seen a brighter day dawning for the church. But encouragement had changed to reproach and condemnation. Many dignitaries, of both church and state, were convicted of the truthfulness of his theses; but they soon saw that the acceptance of these truths would involve great changes. To enlighten and reform the people would be virtually to undermine the authority of Rome, to stop thousands of streams now flowing into her treasury, and thus greatly to curtail the extravagance and luxury of the papal leaders. Furthermore, to teach the people to think and act as responsible beings, looking to Christ alone for salvation, would overthrow the pontiff's throne and eventually destroy their own authority. For this reason they refused the knowledge tendered them of God and arrayed themselves against Christ and the truth by their opposition to the man whom He had sent to enlighten them.

Luther trembled as he looked upon himself—one man opposed to the mightiest powers of earth. He sometimes doubted whether he had indeed been led of God to set himself against the authority of the church. "Who was I," he writes, "to oppose the majesty of the pope, before whom … the kings of the earth and the whole world trembled? … No one can know what my heart suffered during these first two years, and into what despondency, I may say into what despair, I was sunk." —*Ibid.*, b. 3, ch. 6. But he was not left to become utterly disheartened. When human support failed, he looked to God alone and learned that he could lean in perfect safety upon that all-powerful arm.

To a friend of the Reformation Luther wrote: "We cannot attain to the understanding of Scripture either by study or by the intellect. Your first duty is to begin by prayer. Entreat the Lord to grant you, of His great mercy, the true understanding of His word. There is no other interpreter of the word of God than the Author of this word, as He Himself has said, 'They shall be all taught of God.' Hope for nothing from your own labors, from your own understanding: trust solely in God, and in the influence of His Spirit. Believe this on the word of a man who has had experience." —*Ibid.*, b. 3, ch. 7. Here is a lesson of vital importance to those who feel that God has called them to present to others the solemn truths for this time. These truths will stir the enmity of Satan and of men who love the fables that he has devised. In the conflict with the powers of evil there is need of something more than strength of intellect and human wisdom.

When enemies appealed to custom and tradition, or to the assertions and authority of the pope, Luther met them with the Bible and the Bible only. Here were arguments which they could not answer; therefore the slaves of formalism and superstition clamored for his blood, as the Jews had clamored for the blood of Christ. "He is a heretic," cried the Roman zealots. "It is high treason against the church to allow so horrible a heretic to live one hour longer. Let the scaffold be instantly erected for him!" —*Ibid.*, b. 3, ch. 9. But Luther did not fall a prey to their fury. God had a work for him to do, and angels of heaven were sent to protect him. Many, however, who had received from Luther the precious light were made the objects of Satan's wrath and for the truth's sake fearlessly suffered torture and death.

Luther's teachings attracted the attention of thoughtful minds throughout all Germany. From his sermons and writings issued beams of light which awakened and illuminated thousands. A living faith was taking the place of the dead formalism in which the church had so long been held. The people were daily losing confidence in the superstitions of Romanism. The barriers of prejudice were giving way. The word of God, by which Luther tested every doctrine and every claim, was like a two-edged sword, cutting its way to the hearts of the people. Everywhere there was awakening a desire for spiritual progress. Everywhere was such a hungering and thirsting after righteousness as had not been known for ages. The eyes of the people, so long directed to human rites and earthly mediators, were now turning in penitence and faith to Christ and Him crucified.

This widespread interest aroused still further the fears of the papal authorities. Luther received a summons to appear at Rome to answer to the charge of heresy. The command filled his friends with terror. They knew full well the danger that threatened him in that corrupt city, already drunk with the blood of the martyrs of Jesus. They protested against his going to Rome and requested that he receive his examination in Germany.

This arrangement was finally effected, and the pope's legate was appointed to hear the case. In the instructions communicated by the pontiff to this official, it was stated that Luther had already been declared a heretic. The legate was therefore charged "to prosecute and constrain without any delay." If he should remain steadfast, and the legate should fail to gain possession of his person, he was empowered "to proscribe him in every part of Germany; to banish, curse, and excommunicate all those who are attached to him." —*Ibid.*, b. 4, ch. 2. And, further, the pope directed his legate, in order entirely to root out the pestilent heresy, to excommunicate all, of whatever dignity in church or state, except the emperor, who should neglect to seize Luther and his adherents, and deliver them up to the vengeance of Rome.

Here is displayed the true spirit of popery. Not a trace of Christian principle, or even of common justice, is to be seen in the whole document. Luther was at a great distance from Rome; he had had no opportunity to explain or defend his position; yet before his case had been investigated, he was summarily pronounced a heretic, and in the same day, exhorted, accused, judged, and condemned; and all this by the self-styled holy father, the only supreme, infallible authority in church or state!

At this time, when Luther so much needed the sympathy and counsel of a true friend, God's providence sent Melanchthon to Wittenberg. Young in years, modest and diffident in his manners, Melanchthon's sound judgment, extensive knowledge, and winning eloquence, combined with the purity and uprightness of his character, won universal admiration and esteem. The brilliancy of his talents was not more marked than his gentleness of disposition. He soon became an earnest disciple of the gospel, and Luther's most trusted friend and valued supporter; his gentleness, caution, and exactness serving as a complement to Luther's courage and energy. Their union in the work added strength to the Reformation and was a source of great encouragement to Luther.

Augsburg had been fixed upon as the place of trial, and the Reformer set out on foot to perform the journey thither. Serious fears were entertained in his behalf. Threats had been made openly that he would be seized and murdered on the way, and his friends begged him not to venture. They even entreated him to leave Wittenberg for a time and find safety with those who would gladly protect him. But he would not leave the position where God had placed him. He must continue faithfully to maintain the truth, notwithstanding the storms that were beating upon him. His language was: "I am like Jeremiah, a man of strife and contention; but the more their threats increase, the more my joy is multiplied. ... They have already destroyed my honor and my reputation. One single thing remains; it is my wretched body: let them take it; they will thus shorten my life by a few hours. But as for my soul, they cannot take that. He who desires to proclaim the word of Christ to the world, must expect death at every moment." —*Ibid.*, b. 4, ch. 4.

The tidings of Luther's arrival at Augsburg gave great satisfaction to the papal legate. The troublesome heretic who was exciting the attention of the whole world seemed now in the power of Rome, and the legate determined that he should not escape. The Reformer had failed to provide himself with a safe-conduct. His friends urged him not to appear before the legate without one, and they themselves undertook to procure it from the emperor. The legate intended to force Luther, if possible, to retract, or, failing in this, to cause him to be conveyed to Rome, to share the fate of Huss and Jerome. Therefore through his agents he endeavored to induce Luther to appear without a safe-conduct, trusting himself to his mercy. This the Reformer firmly declined to do. Not until he had received the document pledging him the emperor's protection, did he appear in the presence of the papal ambassador.

As a matter of policy, the Romanists had decided to attempt to win Luther by an appearance of gentleness. The legate, in his interviews with him, professed great friendliness; but he demanded that Luther submit implicitly to the authority of the church, and yield every point without argument or question. He had not rightly estimated the character of the man with whom he had to deal. Luther, in reply, expressed his regard for the church, his desire for the truth, his readiness to answer all objections to what he had taught, and to submit his doctrines to the decision of certain leading universities. But at the same time he protested against the cardinal's course in requiring him to retract without having proved him in error.

The only response was: "Retract, retract!" The Reformer showed that his position was sustained by the Scriptures and firmly declared that he could not renounce the truth. The legate, unable to reply to Luther's arguments, overwhelmed him with a storm of reproaches, gibes, and flattery, interspersed with quotations from tradition and the sayings of the Fathers, granting the Reformer no opportunity to speak. Seeing that the conference, thus continued, would be utterly futile, Luther finally obtained a reluctant permission to present his answer in writing.

"In so doing," said he, writing to a friend, "the oppressed find double gain; first, what is written may be submitted to the judgment of others; and second, one has a better chance of working on the fears, if not on the conscience, of an arrogant and babbling despot, who would otherwise overpower by his imperious language." —Martyn, *The Life and Times of Luther*, pages 271, 272.

At the next interview, Luther presented a clear, concise, and forcible exposition of his views, fully supported by many quotations from Scripture. This paper, after reading aloud, he handed to the cardinal, who, however, cast it contemptuously aside, declaring it to be a mass of idle words and irrelevant quotations. Luther, fully aroused, now met the haughty prelate on his own ground—the traditions and teachings of the church—and utterly overthrew his assumptions.

When the prelate saw that Luther's reasoning was unanswerable, he lost all self-control, and in a rage cried out: "Retract! or I will send you to Rome, there to appear before the judges commissioned to take cognizance of your cause. I will excommunicate you and all your partisans, and all who shall at any time countenance you, and will cast them out of the church." And he finally declared, in a haughty and angry tone: "Retract, or return no more." —D'Aubigne, London ed., b. 4, ch. 8.

The Reformer promptly withdrew with his friends, thus declaring plainly that no retraction was to be expected from him. This was not what the cardinal had purposed. He had flattered himself that by violence he could awe Luther to submission. Now, left alone with his supporters, he looked from one to another in utter chagrin at the unexpected failure of his schemes.

Luther's efforts on this occasion were not without good results. The large assembly present had opportunity to compare the two men, and to judge for themselves of the spirit manifested by them, as well as of the strength and truthfulness of their positions. How marked the contrast! The Reformer, simple, humble, firm, stood up in the strength of God, having truth on his side; the pope's representative, self-important, overbearing, haughty, and unreasonable, was without a single argument from the Scriptures, yet vehemently crying: "Retract, or be sent to Rome for punishment."

Notwithstanding Luther had secured a safe-conduct, the Romanists were plotting to seize and imprison him. His friends urged that as it was useless for him to prolong his stay, he should return to Wittenberg without delay, and that the utmost caution should be observed in order to conceal his intentions. He accordingly left Augsburg before daybreak, on horseback, accompanied only by a guide furnished him by the magistrate. With many forebodings he secretly made his way through the dark and silent streets of the city. Enemies, vigilant and cruel, were plotting his destruction. Would he escape the snares prepared for him? Those were moments of anxiety and earnest prayer. He reached a small gate in the wall of the city. It was opened for him, and with his guide he passed through without hindrance. Once safely outside, the fugitives hastened their flight, and before the legate learned of Luther's departure, he was beyond the reach of his persecutors. Satan and his emissaries were defeated. The man whom they had thought in their power was gone, escaped as a bird from the snare of the fowler.

At the news of Luther's escape the legate was overwhelmed with surprise and anger. He had expected to receive great honor for his wisdom and firmness in dealing with this disturber of the church; but his hope was disappointed. He gave expression to his wrath in a letter to Frederick, the elector of Saxony, bitterly denouncing Luther and demanding that Frederick send the Reformer to Rome or banish him from Saxony.

In defense, Luther urged that the legate or the pope show him his errors from the Scriptures, and pledged himself in the most solemn manner to renounce his doctrines if they could be shown to contradict the word of God. And he expressed his gratitude to God that he had been counted worthy to suffer in so holy a cause.

The elector had, as yet, little knowledge of the reformed doctrines, but he was deeply impressed by the candor, force, and clearness of Luther's words; and until the Reformer should be proved to be in error, Frederick resolved to stand as his protector. In reply to the legate's demand he wrote: "Since Dr. Martin has appeared before you at Augsburg, you should be satisfied. We did not expect that you would endeavor to make him retract without having convinced him of his errors. None of the learned men in our principality have informed me that Martin's doctrine is impious, anti-christian, or heretical.' The prince refused, moreover, to send Luther to Rome, or to expel him from his states." —D'Aubigne, b. 4, ch. 10.

The elector saw that there was a general breaking down of the moral restraints of society. A great work of reform was needed. The complicated and expensive arrangements to restrain and punish crime would be unnecessary if men but acknowledged and obeyed the requirements of God and the dictates of an enlightened conscience. He saw that Luther was laboring to secure this object, and he secretly rejoiced that a better influence was making itself felt in the church.

He saw also that as a professor in the university Luther was eminently successful. Only a year had passed since the Reformer posted his theses on the castle church, yet there was already a great falling off in the number of pilgrims that visited the church at the festival of All Saints. Rome had been deprived of worshipers and offerings, but their place was filled by another class, who now came to Wittenberg, not pilgrims to adore her relics, but students to fill her halls of learning. The writings of Luther had kindled everywhere a new interest in the Holy Scriptures, and not only from all parts of Germany, but from other lands, students flocked to the university. Young men, coming in sight of Wittenberg for the first time, "raised their hands to heaven, and praised God for having caused the light of truth to shine forth from this city, as from Zion in times of old, and whence it spread even to the most distant countries." —*Ibid.*, b. 4, ch. 10.

Luther was as yet but partially converted from the errors of Romanism. But as he compared the Holy Oracles with the papal decrees and constitutions, he was filled with wonder. "I am reading," he wrote, "the decrees of the pontiffs, and … I do not know whether the pope is antichrist himself, or his apostle, so greatly is Christ misrepresented and crucified in them." —*Ibid.*, b. 5, ch. 1. Yet at this time Luther was still a supporter of the Roman Church, and had no thought that he would ever separate from her communion.

The Reformer's writings and his doctrine were extending to every nation in Christendom. The work spread to Switzerland and Holland. Copies of his writings found their way to France and Spain. In England his teachings were received as the word of life. To Belgium and Italy also the truth had extended. Thousands were awakening from their deathlike stupor to the joy and hope of a life of faith.

Rome became more and more exasperated by the attacks of Luther, and it was declared by some of his fanatical opponents, even by doctors in Catholic universities, that he who should kill the rebellious monk would be without sin. One day a stranger, with a pistol hidden under his cloak, approached the Reformer and inquired why he went thus alone. "I am in God's hands," answered Luther. "He is my strength and my shield. What can man do unto me?" —*Ibid.*, b. 6, ch. 2. Upon hearing these words, the stranger turned pale and fled away as from the presence of the angels of heaven.

Rome was bent upon the destruction of Luther; but God was his defense. His doctrines were heard everywhere—"in cottages and convents, … in the castles of the nobles, in the universities, and in the palaces of kings;" and noble men were rising on every hand to sustain his efforts. —*Ibid.*, b. 6, ch. 2.

It was about this time that Luther, reading the works of Huss, found that the great truth of justification by faith, which he himself was seeking to uphold and teach, had been held by the Bohemian Reformer. "We have all," said Luther, "Paul, Augustine, and myself, been Hussites without knowing it!" "God will surely visit it upon the world," he continued, "that the truth was preached to it a century ago, and burned!" —Wylie, b. 6. ch. 1

In an appeal to the emperor and nobility of Germany in behalf of the reformation of Christianity, Luther wrote concerning the pope: "It is a horrible thing to behold the man who styles himself Christ's vicegerent, displaying a magnificence that no emperor can equal. Is this being like the poor Jesus, or the humble Peter? He is, say they, the lord of the world! But Christ, whose vicar he boasts of being, has said, 'My kingdom is not of this world.' Can the dominions of a vicar extend beyond those of his superior?" —D'Aubigne, b. 6, ch. 3.

He wrote thus of the universities: "I am much afraid that the universities will prove to be the great gates of hell, unless they diligently labor in explaining the Holy Scriptures, and engraving them in the hearts of youth. I advise no one to place his child where the Scriptures do not reign paramount. Every institution in which men are not unceasingly occupied with the word of God must become corrupt." —*Ibid.*, b. 6, ch. 3.

This appeal was rapidly circulated throughout Germany and exerted a powerful influence upon the people. The whole nation was stirred, and multitudes were roused to rally around the standard of reform. Luther's opponents, burning with a desire for revenge, urged the pope to take decisive measures against him. It was decreed that his doctrines should be immediately condemned. Sixty days were granted the Reformer and his adherents, after which, if they did not recant, they were all to be excommunicated.

That was a terrible crisis for the Reformation. For centuries Rome's sentence of excommunication had struck terror to powerful monarchs; it had filled mighty empires with woe and desolation. Those upon whom its condemnation fell were universally regarded with dread and horror; they were cut off from intercourse with their fellows and treated as outlaws, to be hunted to extermination. Luther was not blind to the tempest about to burst upon him; but he stood firm, trusting in Christ to be his support and shield. With a martyr's faith and courage he wrote: "What is about to happen I know not, nor do I care to know. ... Let the blow light where it may, I am without fear. Not so much as a leaf falls, without the will of our Father. How much rather will He care for us! It is a light thing to die for the Word, since the Word which was made flesh hath Himself died. If we die with Him, we shall live with Him; and passing through that which He has passed through before us, we shall be where He is and dwell with Him forever." —*Ibid.*, 3d London ed., Walther, 1840, b. 6, ch. 9.

When the papal bull reached Luther, he said: "I despise and attack it, as impious, false. ... It is *Christ* Himself who is condemned therein. ... I rejoice in having to bear such ills for the best of causes. Already I feel greater liberty in my heart; for at last I know that the pope is antichrist, and that his throne is that of Satan himself." —D'Aubigne, b. 6, ch. 9.

Yet the mandate of Rome was not without effect. Prison, torture, and sword were weapons potent to enforce obedience. The weak and superstitious trembled before the decree of the pope; and while there was general sympathy for Luther, many felt that life was too dear to be risked in the cause of reform. Everything seemed to indicate that the Reformer's work was about to close.

But Luther was fearless still. Rome had hurled her anathemas against him, and the world looked on, nothing doubting that he would perish or be forced to yield. But with terrible power he flung back upon herself the sentence of condemnation and publicly declared his determination to abandon her forever. In the presence of a crowd of students, doctors, and citizens of all ranks Luther burned the pope's bull, with the canon laws, the decretals, and certain writings sustaining the papal power. "My enemies have been able, by burning my books," he said, "to injure the cause of truth in the minds of the common people, and destroy their souls; for this reason I consumed their books in return. A serious struggle has just begun. Hitherto I have been only playing with the pope. I began this work in God's name; it will be ended without me, and by His might." —*Ibid.*, b. 6, ch. 10.

To the reproaches of his enemies who taunted him with the weakness of his cause, Luther answered: "Who knows if God has not chosen and called me, and if they ought not to fear that, by despising me, they despise God Himself? Moses was alone at the departure from Egypt; Elijah was alone in the reign of King Ahab; Isaiah alone in Jerusalem; Ezekiel alone in Babylon. … God never selected as a prophet either the high priest or any other great personage; but ordinarily He chose low and despised men, once even the shepherd Amos. In every age, the saints have had to reprove the great, kings, princes, priests, and wise men, at the peril of their lives. … I do not say that I am a prophet; but I say that they ought to fear precisely because I am alone and that they are many. I am sure of this, that the word of God is with me, and that it is not with them." —*Ibid.*, b. 6, ch. 10.

Yet it was not without a terrible struggle with himself that Luther decided upon a final separation from the church. It was about this time that he wrote: "I feel more and more every day how difficult it is to lay aside the scruples which one has imbibed in childhood. Oh, how much pain it has caused me, though I had the Scriptures on my side, to justify it to myself that I should dare to make a stand alone against the pope, and hold him forth as antichrist! What have the tribulations of my heart not been! How many times have I not asked myself with bitterness that question which was so frequent on the lips of the papists: 'Art thou alone wise? Can everyone else be mistaken? How will it be, if, after all, it is thyself who art wrong, and who art involving in thy error so many souls, who will then be eternally damned?' 'Twas so I fought with myself and with Satan, till Christ, by His own infallible word, fortified my heart against these doubts." —Martyn, pages 372, 373.

The pope had threatened Luther with excommunication if he did not recant, and the threat was now fulfilled. A new bull appeared, declaring the Reformer's final separation from the Roman Church, denouncing him as accursed of Heaven, and including in the same condemnation all who should receive his doctrines. The great contest had been fully entered upon.

Opposition is the lot of all whom God employs to present truths specially applicable to their time. There was a present truth in the days of Luther,—a truth at that time of special importance; there is a present truth for the church today. He who does all things according to the counsel of His will has been pleased to place men under various circumstances and to enjoin upon them duties peculiar to the times in which they live and the conditions under which they are placed. If they would prize the light given them, broader views of truth would be opened before them. But truth is no more desired by the majority today than it was by the papists who opposed Luther. There is the same disposition to accept the theories and traditions of men instead of the word of God as in former ages. Those who present the truth for this time should not expect to be received with greater favor than were earlier reformers. The great controversy between truth and error, between Christ and Satan, is to increase in intensity to the close of this world's history.

Said Jesus to His disciples: "If ye were of the world, the world would love his own: but because ye are not of the world, but I have chosen you out of the world, therefore the world hateth you. Remember the word that I said unto you, The servant is not greater than his Lord. If they have persecuted Me, they will also persecute you; if they have kept My saying, they will keep yours also." John 15:19, 20. And on the other hand our Lord declared plainly: "Woe unto you, when all men shall speak well of you! for so did their fathers to the false prophets." Luke 6:26. The spirit of the world is no more in harmony with the spirit of Christ today than in earlier times, and those who preach the word of God in its purity will be received with no greater favor now than then. The forms of opposition to the truth may change, the enmity may be less open because it is more subtle; but the same antagonism still exists and will be manifested to the end of time.

Five

—Luther Before the Diet—

A new emperor, Charles V, had ascended the throne of Germany, and the emissaries of Rome hastened to present their congratulations and induce the monarch to employ his power against the Reformation. On the other hand, the elector of Saxony, to whom Charles was in great degree indebted for his crown, entreated him to take no step against Luther until he should have granted him a hearing. The emperor was thus placed in a position of great perplexity and embarrassment. The papists would be satisfied with nothing short of an imperial edict sentencing Luther to death. The elector had declared firmly that "neither his imperial majesty nor any other person had shown that Luther's writings had been refuted;" therefore he requested "that Dr. Luther should be furnished with a safe-conduct, so that he might appear before a tribunal of learned, pious, and impartial judges." —D'Aubigne, b. 6, ch. 11.

The attention of all parties was now directed to the assembly of the German states which convened at Worms soon after the accession of Charles to the empire. There were important political questions and interests to be considered by this national council; for the first time the princes of Germany were to meet their youthful monarch in deliberative assembly. From all parts of the fatherland had come the dignitaries of church and state. Secular lords, highborn, powerful, and jealous of their hereditary rights; princely ecclesiastics, flushed with their conscious superiority in rank and power; courtly knights and their armed retainers; and ambassadors from foreign and distant lands,—all gathered at Worms. Yet in that vast assembly the subject that excited the deepest interest was the cause of the Saxon Reformer.

Charles had previously directed the elector to bring Luther with him to the Diet, assuring him of protection, and promising a free discussion, with competent persons, of the questions in dispute. Luther was anxious to appear before the emperor. His health was at this time much impaired; yet he wrote to the elector: "If I cannot go to Worms in good health, I will be carried there, sick as I am. For if the emperor calls me, I cannot doubt that it is the call of God Himself. If they desire to use violence against me, and that is very probable (for it is not for their instruction that they order me to appear), I place the matter in the Lord's hands. He still lives and reigns who preserved the three young men in the burning fiery furnace. If He will not save me, my life is of little consequence. Let us only prevent the gospel from being exposed to the scorn of the wicked, and let us shed our blood for it, for fear they should triumph. It is not for me to decide whether my life or my death will contribute most to the salvation of all. … You may expect everything from me … except flight and recantation. Fly I cannot, and still less retract." —*Ibid.*, b. 7, ch. 1.

As the news was circulated at Worms that Luther was to appear before the Diet, a general excitement was created. Aleander, the papal legate to whom the case had been specially entrusted, was alarmed and enraged. He saw that the result would be disastrous to the papal cause. To institute inquiry into a case in which the pope had already pronounced sentence of condemnation would be to cast contempt upon the authority of the sovereign pontiff. Furthermore, he was apprehensive that the eloquent and powerful arguments of this man might turn away many of the princes from the cause of the pope. He therefore, in the most urgent manner, remonstrated with Charles against Luther's appearance at Worms. About this time the bull declaring Luther's excommunication was published; and this, coupled with the representations of the legate, induced the emperor to yield. He wrote to the elector that if Luther would not retract, he must remain at Wittenberg.

Not content with this victory, Aleander labored with all the power and cunning at his command to secure Luther's condemnation. With a persistence worthy of a better cause, he urged the matter upon the attention of princes, prelates, and other members of the assembly, accusing the Reformer of "sedition, rebellion, impiety, and blasphemy." But the vehemence and passion manifested by the legate revealed too plainly the spirit by which he was actuated. "He is moved by hatred and vengeance," was the general remark, "much more than by zeal and piety." —*Ibid.*, b. 7, ch. 1. The majority of the Diet were more than ever inclined to regard Luther's cause with favor.

With redoubled zeal Aleander urged upon the emperor the duty of executing the papal edicts. But under the laws of Germany this could not be done without the concurrence of the princes; and, overcome at last by the legate's importunity, Charles bade him present his case to the Diet. "It was a proud day for the nuncio. The assembly was a great one: the cause was even greater. Aleander was to plead for Rome, … the mother and mistress of all churches." He was to vindicate the princedom of Peter before the assembled principalities of Christendom. "He had the gift of eloquence, and he rose to the greatness of the occasion. Providence ordered it that Rome should appear and plead by the ablest of her orators in the presence of the most august of tribunals, before she was condemned." —Wylie, b. 6, ch. 4. With some misgivings those who favored the Reformer looked forward to the effect of Aleander's speech. The elector of Saxony was not present, but by his direction some of his councilors attended to take notes of the nuncio's address.

With all the power of learning and eloquence, Aleander set himself to over-throw the truth. Charge after charge he hurled against Luther as an enemy of the church and the state, the living and the dead, clergy and laity, councils and private Christians. "In Luther's errors there is enough," he declared, to warrant the burning of "a hundred thousand heretics."

In conclusion he endeavored to cast contempt upon the adherents of the reformed faith: "What are all these Lutherans? A crew of insolent pedagogues, corrupt priests, dissolute monks, ignorant lawyers, and degraded nobles, with the common people whom they have misled and perverted. How far superior to them is the Catholic party in number, ability, and power! A unanimous decree from this illustrious assembly will enlighten the simple, warn the imprudent, decide the waverers, and give strength to the weak." —D'Aubigne, b. 7, ch. 3.

With such weapons the advocates of truth in every age have been attacked. The same arguments are still urged against all who dare to present, in opposition to established errors, the plain and direct teachings of God's word. "Who are these preachers of new doctrines?" exclaim those who desire a popular religion. "They are unlearned, few in numbers, and of the poorer class. Yet they claim to have the truth, and to be the chosen people of God. They are ignorant and deceived. How greatly superior in numbers and influence is our church! How many great and learned men are among us! How much more power is on our side!" These are the arguments that have a telling influence upon the world; but they are no more conclusive now than in the days of the Reformer.

The Reformation did not, as many suppose, end with Luther. It is to be continued to the close of this world's history. Luther had a great work to do in reflecting to others the light which God had permitted to shine upon him; yet he did not receive all the light which was to be given to the world. From that time to this, new light has been continually shining upon the Scriptures, and new truths have been constantly unfolding.

The legate's address made a deep impression upon the Diet. There was no Luther present, with the clear and convincing truths of God's word, to vanquish the papal champion. No attempt was made to defend the Reformer. There was manifest a general disposition not only to condemn him and the doctrines which he taught, but if possible to uproot the heresy. Rome had enjoyed the most favorable opportunity to defend her cause. All that she could say in her own vindication had been said. But the apparent victory was the signal of defeat. Henceforth the contrast between truth and error would be more clearly seen, as they should take the field in open warfare. Never from that day would Rome stand as secure as she had stood.

While most of the members of the Diet would not have hesitated to yield up Luther to the vengeance of Rome, many of them saw and deplored the existing depravity in the church, and desired a suppression of the abuses suffered by the

German people in consequence of the corruption and greed of the hierarchy. The legate had presented the papal rule in the most favorable light. Now the Lord moved upon a member of the Diet to give a true delineation of the effects of papal tyranny. With noble firmness, Duke George of Saxony stood up in that princely assembly and specified with terrible exactness the deceptions and abominations of popery, and their dire results. In closing he said:

"These are some of the abuses that cry out against Rome. All shame has been put aside, and their only object is ...money, money, money, ... so that the preachers who should teach the truth, utter nothing but falsehoods, and are not only tolerated, but rewarded, because the greater their lies, the greater their gain. It is from this foul spring that such tainted waters flow. Debauchery stretches out the hand to avarice. ... Alas, it is the scandal caused by the clergy that hurls so many poor souls into eternal condemnation. A general reform must be effected." —*Ibid.*, b. 7, ch. 4.

A more able and forcible denunciation of the papal abuses could not have been presented by Luther himself; and the fact that the speaker was a determined enemy of the Reformer's gave greater influence to his words.

Had the eyes of the assembly been opened, they would have beheld angels of God in the midst of them, shedding beams of light athwart the darkness of error and opening minds and hearts to the reception of truth. It was the power of the God of truth and wisdom that controlled even the adversaries of the reformation, and thus prepared the way for the great work about to be accomplished. Martin Luther was not present; but the voice of One greater than Luther had been heard in that assembly.

A committee was at once appointed by the Diet to prepare an enumeration of the papal oppressions that weighed so heavily on the German people. This list, containing a hundred and one specifications, was presented to the emperor, with a request that he would take immediate measures for the correction of these abuses. "What a loss of Christian souls," said the petitioners, "what depredations, what extortions, on account of the scandals by which the spiritual head of Christendom is surrounded! It is our duty to prevent the ruin and dishonor of our people. For this reason we most humbly but most urgently entreat you to order a general reformation, and to undertake its accomplishment." —Ibid b. 7, ch. 4.

The council now demanded the Reformer's appearance before them. Notwithstanding the entreaties, protests, and threats of Aleander, the emperor at last consented, and Luther was summoned to appear before the Diet. With the summons was issued a safe-conduct, ensuring his return to a place of security. These were borne to Wittenberg by a herald, who was commissioned to conduct him to Worms.

The friends of Luther were terrified and distressed. Knowing the prejudice and enmity against him, they feared that even his safe-conduct would not be respected, and they entreated him not to imperil his life. He replied: "The papists do not desire my coming to Worms, but my condemnation and my death. It matters not. Pray not for me, but for the word of God. ... Christ will give me His Spirit to overcome these ministers of error. I despise them during my life; I shall triumph over them by my death. They are busy at Worms about compelling me to retract; and this shall be my retraction: I said formerly that the pope was Christ's vicar; now I assert that he is our Lord's adversary, and the devil's apostle." —Ibid b. 7, ch. 6.

Luther was not to make his perilous journey alone. Besides the imperial messenger, three of his firmest friends determined to accompany him. Melanchthon earnestly desired to join them. His heart was knit to Luther's, and he yearned to follow him, if need be, to prison or to death. But his entreaties were denied. Should Luther perish, the hopes of the Reformation must center upon his youthful colaborer. Said the Reformer as he parted from Melanchthon: "If I do not return, and my enemies put me to death, continue to teach, and stand fast in the truth. Labor in my stead. ... If you survive, my death will be of little consequence." —Ibid b. 7, ch. 7. Students and citizens who had gathered to witness Luther's departure were deeply moved. A multitude whose hearts had been touched by the gospel, bade him farewell with weeping. Thus the Reformer and his companions set out from Wittenberg.

On the journey they saw that the minds of the people were oppressed by gloomy forebodings. At some towns no honors were proffered them. As they stopped for the night, a friendly priest expressed his fears by holding up before Luther the portrait of an Italian reformer who had suffered martyrdom. The next day they learned that Luther's writings had been condemned at Worms. Imperial messengers were proclaiming the emperor's decree and calling upon the people to bring the proscribed works to the magistrates. The herald, fearing for Luther's safety at the council, and thinking that already his resolution might be shaken, asked if he still wished to go forward. He answered: "Although interdicted in every city, I shall go on." —Ibid b. 7, ch. 7.

At Erfurt, Luther was received with honor. Surrounded by admiring crowds, he passed through the streets that he had often traversed with his beggar's wallet. He visited his convent cell, and thought upon the struggles through which the light now flooding Germany had been shed upon his soul. He was urged to preach. This he had been forbidden to do, but the herald granted him permission, and the friar who had once been made the drudge of the convent, now entered the pulpit.

To a crowded assembly he spoke from the words of Christ, "Peace be unto you." "Philosophers, doctors, and writers," he said, "have endeavored to teach men the way to obtain everlasting life, and they have not succeeded. I will now tell it to you: ... God has raised one Man from the dead, the Lord Jesus Christ, that He might destroy death, extirpate sin, and shut the gates of hell. This is the work of salvation. ... Christ has vanquished! this is the joyful news; and we are saved by His work, and not by our own. ... Our Lord Jesus Christ said, 'Peace be unto you; behold My hands;' that is to say, Behold, O man! it is I, I alone, who have taken away thy sin, and ransomed thee; and now thou hast peace, saith the Lord."

He continued, showing that true faith will be manifested by a holy life. "Since God has saved us, let us so order our works that they may be acceptable to Him. Art thou rich? let thy goods administer to the necessities of the poor. Art thou poor? let thy services be acceptable to the rich. If thy labor is useful to thyself alone, the service that thou pretendest to render unto God is a lie." —*Ibid* b. 7, ch. 7.

The people listened as if spellbound. The bread of life was broken to those starving souls. Christ was lifted up before them as above popes, legates, emperors, and kings. Luther made no reference to his own perilous position. He did not seek to make himself the object of thought or sympathy. In the contemplation of Christ he had lost sight of self. He hid behind the Man of Calvary, seeking only to present Jesus as the sinner's Redeemer.

As the Reformer proceeded on his journey, he was everywhere regarded with great interest. An eager multitude thronged about him, and friendly voices warned him of the purpose of the Romanists. "They will burn you," said some, "and reduce your body to ashes, as they did with John Huss." Luther answered, "Though they should kindle a fire all the way from Worms to Wittenberg, the flames of which reached to heaven, I would walk through it in the name of the Lord; I would appear before them; I would enter the jaws of this behemoth, and break his teeth, confessing the Lord Jesus Christ." —*Ibid* b. 7, ch. 7.

The news of his approach to Worms created great commotion. His friends trembled for his safety; his enemies feared for the success of their cause. Strenuous efforts were made to dissuade him from entering the city. At the instigation of the papists he was urged to repair to the castle of a friendly knight, where, it was declared, all difficulties could be amicably adjusted. Friends endeavored to excite his fears by describing the dangers that threatened him. All their efforts failed. Luther, still unshaken, declared: "Even should there be as many devils in Worms as tiles on the housetops, still I would enter it." —*Ibid* b. 7, ch. 7.

Upon his arrival at Worms, a vast crowd flocked to the gates to welcome him. So great a concourse had not assembled to greet the emperor himself. The excitement was intense, and from the midst of the throng a shrill and plaintive voice chanted a funeral dirge as a warning to Luther of the fate that awaited him. "God will be my defense," said he, as he alighted from his carriage.

The papists had not believed that Luther would really venture to appear at Worms, and his arrival filled them with consternation. The emperor immediately summoned his councilors to consider what course should be pursued. One of the bishops, a rigid papist, declared: "We have long consulted on this matter. Let your imperial majesty get rid of this man at once. Did not Sigismund cause John Huss to be burnt? We are not bound either to give or to observe the safe-conduct of a heretic." "No," said the emperor, "we must keep our promise." —*Ibid.*, b. 7, ch. 8. It was therefore decided that the Reformer should be heard.

All the city were eager to see this remarkable man, and a throng of visitors soon filled his lodgings. Luther had scarcely recovered from his recent illness; he was wearied from the journey, which had occupied two full weeks; he must prepare to meet the momentous events of the morrow, and he needed quiet and repose. But so great was the desire to see him that he had enjoyed only a few hours' rest when noblemen, knights, priests, and citizens gathered eagerly about him. Among these were many of the nobles who had so boldly demanded of the emperor a reform of ecclesiastical abuses and who, says Luther, "had all been freed by my gospel." —Martyn, page 393. Enemies, as well as friends, came to look upon the dauntless monk; but he received them with unshaken calmness, replying to all with dignity and wisdom. His bearing was firm and courageous. His pale, thin face, marked with the traces of toil and illness, wore a kindly and even joyous expression. The solemnity and deep earnestness of his words gave him a power that even his enemies could not wholly withstand. Both friends and foes were filled with wonder. Some were convinced that a divine influence attended him; others declared, as had the Pharisees concerning Christ: "He hath a devil."

On the following day Luther was summoned to attend the Diet. An imperial officer was appointed to conduct him to the hall of audience; yet it was with difficulty that he reached the place. Every avenue was crowded with spectators eager to look upon the monk who had dared resist the authority of the pope.

As he was about to enter the presence of his judges, an old general, the hero of many battles, said to him kindly: "Poor monk, poor monk, thou art now going to make a nobler stand than I or any other captains have ever made in the bloodiest of our battles. But if thy cause is just, and thou art sure of it, go forward in God's name, and fear nothing. God will not forsake thee." —D'Aubigne, b. 7, ch. 8.

At length Luther stood before the council. The emperor occupied the throne. He was surrounded by the most illustrious personages in the empire. Never had any man appeared in the presence of a more imposing assembly than that before which Martin Luther was to answer for his faith. "This appearance was of itself a signal victory over the papacy. The pope had condemned the man, and he was now standing before a tribunal which, by this very act, set itself above the pope. The pope had laid him under an interdict, and cut him off from all human society; and yet he was summoned in respectful language, and received before the most august assembly in the world. The pope had condemned him to perpetual silence, and he was now about to speak before thousands of attentive hearers drawn together from the farthest parts of Christendom. An immense revolution had thus been effected by Luther's instrumentality. Rome was already descending from her throne, and it was the voice of a monk that caused this humiliation." —*Ibid.*, b. 7, ch. 8.

In the presence of that powerful and titled assembly the lowly born Reformer seemed awed and embarrassed. Several of the princes, observing his emotion, approached him, and one of them whispered: "Fear not them which kill the body, but are not able to kill the soul." Another said: "When ye shall be brought before governors and kings for My sake, it shall be given you, by the Spirit of your Father, what ye shall say." Thus the words of Christ were brought by the world's great men to strengthen His servant in the hour of trial.

Luther was conducted to a position directly in front of the emperor's throne. A deep silence fell upon the crowded assembly. Then an imperial officer arose and, pointing to a collection of Luther's writings, demanded that the Reformer answer two questions—whether he acknowledged them as his, and whether he proposed to retract the opinions which he had therein advanced. The titles of the books having been read, Luther replied that as to the first question, he acknowledged the books to be his. "As to the second," he said, "seeing that it is a question which concerns faith and the salvation of souls, and in which the word of God, the greatest and most precious treasure either in heaven or earth, is involved, I should act imprudently were I to reply without reflection. I might affirm less than the circumstance demands, or more than truth requires, and so sin against this saying of Christ: 'Whosoever shall deny Me before men, him will I also deny before My Father which is in heaven.' [Matthew 10:33.] For this reason I entreat your imperial majesty, with all humility, to allow me time, that I may answer without offending against the word of God." —D'Aubigne, b. 7, ch. 8.

In making this request, Luther moved wisely. His course convinced the assembly that he did not act from passion or impulse. Such calmness and self-command, unexpected in one who had shown himself bold and uncompromising, added to his power, and enabled him afterward to answer with a prudence, decision, wisdom, and dignity that surprised and disappointed his adversaries, and rebuked their insolence and pride.

The next day he was to appear to render his final answer. For a time his heart sank within him as he contemplated the forces that were combined against the truth. His faith faltered; fearfulness and trembling came upon him, and horror overwhelmed him. Dangers multiplied before him; his enemies seemed about to triumph, and the powers of darkness to prevail. Clouds gathered about him and seemed to separate him from God. He longed for the assurance that the

Lord of hosts would be with him. In anguish of spirit he threw himself with his face upon the earth and poured out those broken, heart-rending cries, which none but God can fully understand.

"O almighty and everlasting God," he pleaded, "how terrible is this world! Behold, it openeth its mouth to swallow me up, and I have so little trust in Thee. … If it is only in the strength of this world that I must put my trust, all is over. … My last hour is come, my condemnation has been pronounced. … O God, do Thou help me against all the wisdom of the world. Do this, … Thou alone; … for this is not my work, but Thine. I have nothing to do here, nothing to contend for with these great ones of the world. … But the cause is Thine, … and it is a righteous and eternal cause. O Lord, help me! Faithful and unchangeable God, in no man do I place my trust. … All that is of man is uncertain; all that cometh of man fails. … Thou hast chosen me for this work. … Stand at my side, for the sake of Thy well-beloved Jesus Christ, who is my defense, my shield, and my strong tower." —*Ibid.*, b. 7, ch. 8.

An all-wise Providence had permitted Luther to realize his peril, that he might not trust to his own strength and rush presumptuously into danger. Yet it was not the fear of personal suffering, a dread of torture or death, which seemed immediately impending, that overwhelmed him with its terror. He had come to the crisis, and he felt his insufficiency to meet it. Through his weakness the cause of truth might suffer loss. Not for his own safety, but for the triumph of the gospel did he wrestle with God. Like Israel's, in that night struggle beside the lonely stream, was the anguish and conflict of his soul. Like Israel, he prevailed with God. In his utter helplessness his faith fastened upon Christ, the mighty Deliverer. He was strengthened with the assurance that he would not appear alone before the council. Peace returned to his soul, and he rejoiced that he was permitted to uplift the word of God before the rulers of the nations.

With his mind stayed upon God, Luther prepared for the struggle before him. He thought upon the plan of his answer, examined passages in his own writings, and drew from the Holy Scriptures suitable proofs to sustain his positions. Then, laying his left hand on the Sacred Volume, which was open before him, he lifted his right hand to heaven and vowed "to remain faithful to the gospel, and freely to confess his faith, even should he seal his testimony with his blood." —*Ibid.*, b. 7, ch. 8.

When he was again ushered into the presence of the Diet, his countenance bore no trace of fear or embarrassment. Calm and peaceful, yet grandly brave and noble, he stood as God's witness among the great ones of the earth. The imperial officer now demanded his decision as to whether he desired to retract his doctrines. Luther made his answer in a subdued and humble tone, without violence or passion. His demeanor was diffident and respectful; yet he manifested a confidence and joy that surprised the assembly.

"Most serene emperor, illustrious princes, gracious lords," said Luther, "I appear before you this day, in conformity with the order given me yesterday, and by God's mercies I conjure your majesty and your august highnesses to listen graciously to the defense of a cause which I am assured is just and true. If, through ignorance, I should transgress the usages and proprieties of courts, I entreat you to pardon me; for I was not brought up in the palaces of kings, but in the seclusion of a convent." —*Ibid.*, b. 7, ch. 8.

Then, proceeding to the question, he stated that his published works were not all of the same character. In some he had treated of faith and good works, and even his enemies declared them not only harmless but profitable. To retract these would be to condemn truths which all parties confessed. The second class consisted of writings exposing the corruptions and abuses of the papacy. To revoke these works would strengthen the tyranny of Rome and open a wider door to many and great impieties. In the third class of his books he had attacked individuals who had defended existing evils. Concerning these he freely confessed that he had been more violent than was becoming. He did not claim to be free from fault; but even these books he could not revoke, for such a course would embolden the enemies of truth, and they would then take occasion to crush God's people with still greater cruelty.

"Yet I am but a mere man, and not God," he continued; "I shall therefore defend myself as Christ did: 'If I have spoken evil, bear witness of the evil.' … By the mercy of God, I conjure you, most serene emperor, and you, most illustrious princes, and all men of every degree, to prove from the writings of the prophets and apostles that I have erred. As soon as I am convinced of this, I will retract every error, and be the first to lay hold of my books and throw them into the fire.

"What I have just said plainly shows, I hope, that I have carefully weighed and considered the dangers to which I expose myself; but far from being dismayed, I rejoice to see that the gospel is now, as in former times, a cause of trouble and dissension. This is the character, this is the destiny, of the word of God. 'I came not to send peace on earth, but a sword,' said Jesus Christ. God is wonderful and terrible in His counsels; beware lest, by presuming to quench dissensions, you should persecute the holy word of God, and draw down upon yourselves a frightful deluge of insurmountable dangers, of present disasters, and eternal desolation. … I might quote many examples from the oracles of God. I might speak of the Pharaohs, the kings of Babylon, and those of Israel, whose labors never more effectually contributed to their own destruction than when they sought by counsels, to all appearance most wise, to strengthen their dominion. 'God removeth mountains, and they know it not.'" —*Ibid.*, b. 7, ch. 8.

Luther had spoken in German; he was now requested to repeat the same words in Latin. Though exhausted by the previous effort, he complied, and again delivered his speech, with the same clearness and energy as at the first. God's providence directed in this matter. The minds of many of the princes were so blinded by error and superstition that at the first delivery they did not see the force of Luther's reasoning; but the repetition enabled them to perceive clearly the points presented.

Those who stubbornly closed their eyes to the light, and determined not to be convinced of the truth, were enraged at the power of Luther's words. As he ceased speaking, the spokesman of the Diet said angrily: "You have not answered the question put to you. ... You are required to give a clear and precise answer. ... Will you, or will you not, retract?"

The Reformer answered: "Since your most serene majesty and your high mightinesses require from me a clear, simple, and precise answer, I will give you one, and it is this: I cannot submit my faith either to the pope or to the councils, because it is clear as the day that they have frequently erred and contradicted each other. Unless therefore I am convinced by the testimony of Scripture or by the clearest reasoning, unless I am persuaded by means of the passages I have quoted, and unless they thus render my conscience bound by the word of God, *I cannot and I will not retract*, for it is unsafe for a Christian to speak against his conscience. Here I stand, I can do no other; may God help me. Amen." —*Ibid.*, b. 7, ch. 8.

Thus stood this righteous man upon the sure foundation of the word of God. The light of heaven illuminated his countenance. His greatness and purity of character, his peace and joy of heart, were manifest to all as he testified against the power of error and witnessed to the superiority of that faith that overcomes the world.

The whole assembly were for a time speechless with amazement. At his first answer Luther had spoken in a low tone, with a respectful, almost submissive bearing. The Romanists had interpreted this as evidence that his courage was beginning to fail. They regarded the request for delay as merely the prelude to his recantation. Charles himself, noting, half contemptuously, the monk's worn frame, his plain attire, and the simplicity of his address, had declared: "This monk will never make a heretic of me." The courage and firmness which he now displayed, as well as the power and clearness of his reasoning, filled all parties with surprise. The emperor, moved to admiration, exclaimed: "This monk speaks with an intrepid heart and unshaken courage." Many of the German princes looked with pride and joy upon this representative of their nation.

The partisans of Rome had been worsted; their cause appeared in a most unfavorable light. They sought to maintain their power, not by appealing to the Scriptures, but by a resort to threats, Rome's unfailing argument. Said the spokesman of the Diet: "If you do not retract, the emperor and the states of the empire will consult what course to adopt against an incorrigible heretic."

Luther's friends, who had with great joy listened to his noble defense, trembled at these words; but the doctor himself said calmly: "May God be my helper, for I can retract nothing." —*Ibid.*, b. 7, ch. 8.

He was directed to withdraw from the Diet while the princes consulted together. It was felt that a great crisis had come. Luther's persistent refusal to submit might affect the history of the church for ages. It was decided to give him one more opportunity to retract. For the last time he was brought into the assembly. Again the question was put, whether he would renounce his doctrines. "I have no other reply to make," he said, "than that which I have already made." It was evident that he could not be induced, either by promises or threats, to yield to the mandate of Rome.

The papal leaders were chagrined that their power, which had caused kings and nobles to tremble, should be thus despised by a humble monk; they longed to make him feel their wrath by torturing his life away. But Luther, understanding his danger, had spoken to all with Christian dignity and calmness. His words had been free from pride, passion, and misrepresentation. He had lost sight of himself, and the great men surrounding him, and felt only that he was in the presence of One infinitely superior to popes, prelates, kings, and emperors. Christ had spoken through Luther's testimony with a power and grandeur that for the time inspired both friends and foes with awe and wonder. The Spirit of God had been present in that council, impressing the hearts of the chiefs of the empire. Several of the princes boldly acknowledged the justice of Luther's cause. Many were convinced of the truth; but with some the impressions received were not lasting. There was another class who did not at the time express their convictions, but who, having searched the Scriptures for themselves, at a future time became fearless supporters of the Reformation.

The elector Frederick had looked forward anxiously to Luther's appearance before the Diet, and with deep emotion he listened to his speech. With joy and pride he witnessed the doctor's courage, firmness, and self-possession, and determined to stand more firmly in his defense. He contrasted the parties in contest, and saw that the wisdom of popes, kings, and prelates had been brought to nought by the power of truth. The papacy had sustained a defeat which would be felt among all nations and in all ages.

As the legate perceived the effect produced by Luther's speech, he feared, as never before, for the security of the Romish power, and resolved to employ every means at his command to effect the Reformer's overthrow. With all the eloquence and diplomatic skill for which he was so eminently distinguished, he represented to the youthful emperor the folly and danger of sacrificing, in the cause of an insignificant monk, the friendship and support of the powerful see of Rome.

His words were not without effect. On the day following Luther's answer, Charles caused a message to be presented to the Diet, announcing his determination to carry out the policy of his predecessors to maintain and protect the Catholic religion. Since Luther had refused to renounce his errors, the most vigorous measures should be employed against him and the heresies he taught. "A single monk, misled by his own folly, has risen against the faith of Christendom. To stay such impiety, I will sacrifice my kingdoms, my treasures, my friends, my body, my blood, my soul, and my life. I am about to dismiss the Augustine Luther, forbidding him to cause the least disorder among the people; I shall then proceed against him and his adherents as contumacious heretics, by excommunication, by interdict, and by every means calculated to destroy them. I call on the members of the states to behave like faithful Christians." —*Ibid.*, b. 7, ch. 9. Nevertheless the emperor declared that Luther's safe-conduct must be respected, and that before proceedings against him could be instituted, he must be allowed to reach his home in safety.

Two conflicting opinions were now urged by the members of the Diet. The emissaries and representatives of the pope again demanded that the Reformer's safe-conduct should be disregarded. "The Rhine," they said, "should receive his ashes, as it had received those of John Huss a century ago." —*Ibid.*, b. 7, ch. 9. But princes of Germany, though themselves papists and avowed enemies to Luther, protested against such a breach of public faith, as a stain upon the honor of the nation. They pointed to the calamities which had followed the death of Huss, and declared that they dared not call down upon Germany, and upon the head of their youthful emperor, a repetition of those terrible evils.

Charles himself, in answer to the base proposal, said: "Though honor and faith should be banished from all the world, they ought to find a refuge in the hearts of princes." —*Ibid* b. 7, ch. 9. He was still further urged by the most bitter of Luther's papal enemies to deal with the Reformer as Sigismund had dealt with Huss—abandon him to the mercies of the church; but recalling the scene when Huss in public assembly had pointed to his chains and reminded the monarch of his plighted faith, Charles V declared: "I should not like to blush like Sigismund." —Lenfant, vol. 1, p. 422.

Yet Charles had deliberately rejected the truths presented by Luther. "I am firmly resolved to imitate the example of my ancestors," wrote the monarch. —D'Aubigne, b. 7, ch. 9. He had decided that he would not step out of the path of custom, even to walk in the ways of truth and righteousness. Because his fathers did, he would uphold the papacy, with all its cruelty and corruption. Thus he took his position, refusing to accept any light in advance of what his fathers had received, or to perform any duty that they had not performed.

There are many at the present day thus clinging to the customs and traditions of their fathers. When the Lord sends them additional light, they refuse to accept it, because, not having been granted to their fathers, it was not received by them. We are not placed where our fathers were; consequently our duties and responsibilities are not the same as theirs. We shall not be approved of God in looking to the example of our fathers to determine our duty instead of searching the word of truth for ourselves. Our responsibility is greater than was that of our ancestors. We are accountable for the light which they received, and which was handed down as an inheritance for us, and we are accountable also for the additional light which is now shining upon us from the word of God.

Said Christ of the unbelieving Jews: "If I had not come and spoken unto them, they had not had sin: but now they have no cloak for their sin." John 15:22. The same divine power had spoken through Luther to the emperor and princes of Germany. And as the light shone forth from God's word, His Spirit pleaded for the last time with many in that assembly. As Pilate, centuries before, permitted pride and popularity to close his heart against the world's Redeemer; as the trembling Felix bade the messenger of truth, "Go thy way for this time; when I have a convenient season, I will call for thee;" as the proud Agrippa confessed, "Almost thou persuadest me to be a Christian" (Acts 24:25; 26:28), yet turned away from the Heaven-sent message—so had Charles V, yielding to the dictates of worldly pride and policy, decided to reject the light of truth.

Rumors of the designs against Luther were widely circulated, causing great excitement throughout the city. The Reformer had made many friends, who, knowing the treacherous cruelty of Rome toward all who dared expose her corruptions, resolved that he should not be sacrificed. Hundreds of nobles pledged themselves to protect him. Not a few openly denounced the royal message as evincing a weak submission to the controlling power of Rome. On the gates of houses and in public places, placards were posted, some condemning and others sustaining Luther. On one of these were written merely the significant words of the wise man: "Woe to thee, O land, when thy king is a child." Ecclesiastes 10:16. The popular enthusiasm in Luther's favor throughout all Germany convinced both the emperor and the Diet that any injustice shown him would endanger the peace of the empire and even the stability of the throne.

Frederick of Saxony maintained a studied reserve, carefully concealing his real feelings toward the Reformer, while at the same time he guarded him with tireless vigilance, watching all his movements and all those of his enemies. But there were many who made no attempt to conceal their sympathy with Luther. He was visited by princes, counts, barons, and other persons of distinction, both lay and ecclesiastical. "The doctor's little room," wrote Spalatin, "could not contain all the visitors who presented themselves." —Martyn, vol. 1, p. 404. The people gazed upon him as if he were more than human. Even those who had no faith in his doctrines could not but admire that lofty integrity which led him to brave death rather than violate his conscience.

Earnest efforts were made to obtain Luther's consent to a compromise with Rome. Nobles and princes represented to him that if he persisted in setting up his own judgment against that of the church and the councils he would soon be banished from the empire and would have no defense. To this appeal Luther answered: "The gospel of Christ cannot be preached without offense. ... Why then should the fear or apprehension of danger separate me from the Lord, and from that divine word which alone is truth? No; I would rather give up my body, my blood, and my life." —D'Aubigne, b. 7, ch. 10.

Again he was urged to submit to the judgment of the emperor, and then he would have nothing to fear. "I consent," said he in reply, "with all my heart, that the emperor, the princes, and even the meanest Christian, should examine and judge my works; but on one condition, that they take the word of God for their standard. Men have nothing to do but to obey it. Do not offer violence to my conscience, which is bound and chained up with the Holy Scriptures." —*Ibid.*, b. 7, ch. 10.

To another appeal he said: "I consent to renounce my safe-conduct. I place my person and my life in the emperor's hands, but the word of God—never!"— *Ibid.*, b. 7, ch. 10. He stated his willingness to submit to the decision of a general council, but only on condition that the council be required to decide according to the Scriptures. "In what concerns the word of God and the faith," he added, "every Christian is as good a judge as the pope, though supported by a million councils, can be for him." —Martyn, vol. 1, p. 410. Both friends and foes were at last convinced that further effort for reconciliation would be useless.

Had the Reformer yielded a single point, Satan and his hosts would have gained the victory. But his unwavering firmness was the means of emancipating the church, and beginning a new and better era. The influence of this one man, who dared to think and act for himself in religious matters, was to affect the church and the world, not only in his own time, but in all future generations. His firmness and fidelity would strengthen all, to the close of time, who should pass through a similar experience. The power and majesty of God stood forth above the counsel of men, above the mighty power of Satan.

Luther was soon commanded by the authority of the emperor to return home, and he knew that this notice would be speedily followed by his condemnation. Threatening clouds overhung his path; but as he departed from Worms, his heart was filled with joy and praise. "The devil himself," said he, "guarded the pope's citadel; but Christ has made a wide breach in it, and Satan was constrained to confess that the Lord is mightier than he." —D'Aubigne, b. 7, ch. 11.

After his departure, still desirous that his firmness should not be mistaken for rebellion, Luther wrote to the emperor. "God, who is the searcher of hearts, is my witness," he said, "that I am ready most earnestly to obey your majesty, in honor or in dishonor, in life or in death, and with no exception save the word of God, by which man lives. In all the affairs of this present life, my fidelity shall be unshaken, for here to lose or to gain is of no consequence to salvation. But when eternal interests are concerned, God wills not that man should submit unto man. For such submission in spiritual matters is a real worship, and ought to be rendered solely to the Creator." —*Ibid.*, b. 7, ch. 11.

On the journey from Worms, Luther's reception was even more flattering than during his progress thither. Princely ecclesiastics welcomed the excommunicated monk, and civil rulers honored the man whom the emperor had denounced. He was urged to preach, and, notwithstanding the imperial prohibition, he again entered the pulpit. "I never pledged myself to chain up the word of God," he said, "nor will I." —Martyn, vol. 1, p. 420.

He had not been long absent from Worms, when the papists prevailed upon the emperor to issue an edict against him. In this decree Luther was denounced as "Satan himself under the form of a man and dressed in a monk's frock." —D'Aubigne, b. 7, ch. 11. It was commanded that as soon as his safe-conduct should expire, measures be taken to stop his work. All persons were forbidden to harbor him, to give him food or drink, or by word or act, in public or private, to aid or abet him. He was to be seized wherever he might be, and delivered to the authorities. His adherents also were to be imprisoned and their property confiscated. His writings were to be destroyed, and, finally, all who should dare to act contrary to this decree were included in its condemnation. The elector of Saxony and the princes most friendly to Luther had left Worms soon after his departure, and the emperor's decree received the sanction of the Diet. Now the Romanists were jubilant. They considered the fate of the Reformation sealed.

God had provided a way of escape for His servant in this hour of peril. A vigilant eye had followed Luther's movements, and a true and noble heart had resolved upon his rescue. It was plain that Rome would be satisfied with nothing short of his death; only by concealment could he be preserved from the jaws of the lion. God gave wisdom to Frederick of Saxony to devise a plan for the Reformer's preservation. With the cooperation of true friends the elector's purpose was carried out, and Luther was effectually hidden from friends and foes. Upon his homeward journey he was seized, separated from his attendants, and hurriedly conveyed through the forest to the castle of Wartburg, an isolated mountain fortress. Both his seizure and his concealment were so involved in mystery that even Frederick himself for a long time knew not whither he had been conducted. This ignorance was not without design; so long as the elector knew nothing of Luther's whereabouts, he could reveal nothing. He satisfied himself that the Reformer was safe, and with this knowledge he was content.

Spring, summer, and autumn passed, and winter came, and Luther still remained a prisoner. Aleander and his partisans exulted as the light of the gospel seemed about to be extinguished. But instead of this, the Reformer was filling his lamp from the storehouse of truth; and its light was to shine forth with brighter radiance.

In the friendly security of the Wartburg, Luther for a time rejoiced in his release from the heat and turmoil of battle. But he could not long find satisfaction in quiet and repose. Accustomed to a life of activity and stern conflict, he could ill endure to remain inactive. In those solitary days the condition of the church rose up before him, and he cried in despair. "Alas! there is no one in this latter day of His anger, to stand like a wall before the Lord, and save Israel!" —*Ibid.*, b. 9, ch. 2. Again, his thoughts returned to himself, and he feared being charged with cowardice in withdrawing from the contest. Then he reproached himself for his indolence and self-indulgence. Yet at the same time he was daily accomplishing more than it seemed possible for one man to do. His pen was never idle. While his enemies flattered themselves that he was silenced, they were astonished and confused by tangible proof that he was still active. A host of tracts, issuing from his pen, circulated throughout Germany. He also performed a most important service for his countrymen by translating the New Testament into the German tongue. From his rocky Patmos he continued for nearly a whole year to proclaim the gospel and rebuke the sins and errors of the times.

But it was not merely to preserve Luther from the wrath of his enemies, nor even to afford him a season of quiet for these important labors, that God had withdrawn His servant from the stage of public life. There were results more precious than these to be secured. In the solitude and obscurity of his mountain retreat, Luther was removed from earthly supports and shut out from human praise. He was thus saved from the pride and self-confidence that are so often caused by success. By suffering and humiliation he was prepared again to walk safely upon the dizzy heights to which he had been so suddenly exalted.

As men rejoice in the freedom which the truth brings them, they are inclined to extol those whom God has employed to break the chains of error and superstition. Satan seeks to divert men's thoughts and affections from God, and to fix them upon human agencies; he leads them to honor the mere instrument and to ignore the Hand that directs all the events of providence. Too often religious leaders who are thus praised and reverenced lose sight of their dependence upon God and are led to trust in themselves. As a result they seek to control the minds and consciences of the people, who are disposed to look to them for guidance instead of looking to the word of God. The work of reform is often retarded because of this spirit indulged by its supporters. From this danger, God would guard the cause of the Reformation. He desired that work to receive, not the impress of man, but that of God. The eyes of men had been turned to Luther as the expounder of the truth; he was removed that all eyes might be directed to the eternal Author of truth.

Six

—The Swiss Reformer—

In the choice of instrumentalities for the reforming of the church, the same divine plan is seen as in that for the planting of the church. The heavenly Teacher passed by the great men of the earth, the titled and wealthy, who were accustomed to receive praise and homage as leaders of the people. They were so proud and self-confident in their boasted superiority that they could not be molded to sympathize with their fellow men and to become colaborers with the humble Man of Nazareth. To the unlearned, toiling fishermen of Galilee was the call addressed: "Follow Me, and I will make you fishers of men." Matthew 4:19. These disciples were humble and teachable. The less they had been influenced by the false teaching of their time, the more successfully could Christ instruct and train them for His service. So in the days of the Great Reformation. The leading Reformers were men from humble life—men who were most free of any of their time from pride of rank and from the influence of bigotry and priestcraft. It is God's plan to employ humble instruments to accomplish great results. Then the glory will not be given to men, but to Him who works through them to will and to do of His own good pleasure.

A few weeks after the birth of Luther in a miner's cabin in Saxony, Ulric Zwingli was born in a herdsman's cottage among the Alps. Zwingli's surroundings in childhood, and his early training, were such as to prepare him for his future mission. Reared amid scenes of natural grandeur, beauty, and awful sublimity, his mind was early impressed with a sense of the greatness, the power, and the majesty of God. The history of the brave deeds achieved upon his native mountains kindled his youthful aspirations. And at the side of his pious grandmother he listened to the few precious Bible stories which she had gleaned from amid the legends and traditions of the church. With eager interest he heard of the grand deeds of patriarchs and prophets, of the shepherds who watched their flocks on the hills of Palestine where angels talked with them, of the Babe of Bethlehem and the Man of Calvary.

Like John Luther, Zwingli's father desired an education for his son, and the boy was early sent from his native valley. His mind rapidly developed, and it soon became a question where to find teachers competent to instruct him. At the age of thirteen he went to Bern, which then possessed the most distinguished school in Switzerland. Here, however, a danger arose which threatened to blight the promise of his life. Determined efforts were put forth by the friars to allure him into a monastery. The Dominican and Franciscan monks were in rivalry for popular favor. This they endeavored to secure by the showy adornments of their churches, the pomp of their ceremonials, and the attractions of famous relics and miracle-working images.

The Dominicans of Bern saw that if they could win this talented young scholar, they would secure both gain and honor. His extreme youth, his natural ability as a speaker and writer, and his genius for music and poetry, would be more effective than all their pomp and display, in attracting the people to their services and increasing the revenues of their order. By deceit and flattery they endeavored to induce Zwingli to enter their convent. Luther, while a student at school, had buried himself in a convent cell, and he would have been lost to the world had not God's providence released him. Zwingli was not permitted to encounter the same peril. Providentially his father received information of the designs of the friars. He had no intention of allowing his son to follow the idle and worthless life of the monks. He saw that his future usefulness was at stake, and directed him to return home without delay.

The command was obeyed; but the youth could not be long content in his native valley, and he soon resumed his studies, repairing, after a time, to Basel. It was here that Zwingli first heard the gospel of God's free grace. Wittembach, a teacher of the ancient languages, had, while studying Greek and Hebrew, been led to the Holy Scriptures, and thus rays of divine light were shed into the minds of the students under his instruction. He declared that there was a truth more ancient, and of infinitely greater worth, than the theories taught by schoolmen and philosophers. This ancient truth was that the death of Christ is the sinner's only ransom. To Zwingli these words were as the first ray of light that precedes the dawn.

Zwingli was soon called from Basel to enter upon his lifework. His first field of labor was in an Alpine parish, not far distant from his native valley. Having received ordination as a priest, he "devoted himself with his whole soul to the search after divine truth; for he was well aware," says a fellow Reformer, "how much he must know to whom the flock of Christ is entrusted." —Wylie, b. 8, ch. 5. The more he searched the Scriptures, the clearer appeared the contrast between their truths and the heresies of Rome. He submitted himself to the Bible as the word of God, the only sufficient, infallible rule. He saw that it must be its own interpreter. He dared not attempt to explain Scripture to sustain a preconceived theory or doctrine, but held it his duty to learn what is its direct and obvious teaching. He sought to avail himself of every help to obtain a full and correct understanding of its meaning, and he invoked the aid of the Holy Spirit, which would, he declared, reveal it to all who sought it in sincerity and with prayer.

"The Scriptures," said Zwingli, "come from God, not from man, and even that God who enlightens will give thee to understand that the speech comes from God. The word of God ... cannot fail; it is bright, it teaches itself, it discloses itself, it illumines the soul with all salvation and grace, comforts it in God, humbles it, so that it loses and even forfeits itself, and embraces God." The truth of these words Zwingli himself had proved. Speaking of his experience at this time, he afterward wrote: "When ... I began to give myself wholly up to the Holy Scriptures, philosophy and theology (scholastic) would always keep suggesting quarrels to me. At last I came to this, that I thought, 'Thou must let all that lie, and learn the meaning of God purely out of His own simple word.' Then I began to ask God for His light, and the Scriptures began to be much easier to me." —*Ibid.*, b. 8, ch. 6.

The doctrine preached by Zwingli was not received from Luther. It was the doctrine of Christ. "If Luther preaches Christ," said the Swiss Reformer, "he does what I am doing. Those whom he has brought to Christ are more numerous than those whom I have led. But this matters not. I will bear no other name than that of Christ, whose soldier I am, and who alone is my Chief. Never has one single word been written by me to Luther, nor by Luther to me. And why?... That it might be shown how much the Spirit of God is in unison with itself, since both of us, without any collusion, teach the doctrine of Christ with such uniformity." —D'Aubigne, b. 8, ch. 9.

In 1516 Zwingli was invited to become a preacher in the convent at Einsiedeln. Here he was to have a closer view of the corruptions of Rome and was to exert an influence as a Reformer that would be felt far beyond his native Alps. Among the chief attractions of Einsiedeln was an image of the Virgin which was said to have the power of working miracles. Above the gateway of the convent was the inscription, "Here a plenary remission of sins may be obtained." —*Ibid.*, b. 8, ch. 5. Pilgrims at all seasons resorted to the shrine of the Virgin; but at the great yearly festival of its consecration multitudes came from all parts of Switzerland, and even from France and Germany. Zwingli, greatly afflicted at the sight, seized the opportunity to proclaim liberty through the gospel to these bondslaves of superstition.

"Do not imagine," he said, "that God is in this temple more than in any other part of creation. Whatever be the country in which you dwell, God is around you, and hears you. ... Can unprofitable works, long pilgrimages, offerings, images, the invocation of the Virgin or of the saints, secure for you the grace of God? ... What avails the multitude of words with which we embody our prayers? What efficacy has a glossy cowl, a smooth-shorn head, a long and flowing robe, or gold-embroidered slippers? ... God looks at the heart, and our hearts are far from Him." "Christ," he said, "who was once offered upon the cross, is the sacrifice and victim, that had made satisfaction for the sins of believers to all eternity." —*Ibid.*, b. 8, ch. 5.

To many listeners these teachings were unwelcome. It was a bitter disappointment to them to be told that their toilsome journey had been made in vain. The pardon freely offered to them through Christ they could not comprehend. They were satisfied with the old way to heaven which Rome had marked out for them. They shrank from the perplexity of searching for anything better. It was easier to trust their salvation to the priests and the pope than to seek for purity of heart.

But another class received with gladness the tidings of redemption through Christ. The observances enjoined by Rome had failed to bring peace of soul, and in faith they accepted the Saviour's blood as their propitiation. These returned to their homes to reveal to others the precious light which they had received. The truth was thus carried from hamlet to hamlet, from town to town, and the number of pilgrims to the Virgin's shrine greatly lessened. There was a falling off in the offerings, and consequently in the salary of Zwingli, which was drawn from them. But this caused him only joy as he saw that the power of fanaticism and superstition was being broken.

The authorities of the church were not blind to the work which Zwingli was accomplishing; but for the present they forbore to interfere. Hoping yet to secure him to their cause, they endeavored to win him by flatteries; and meanwhile the truth was gaining a hold upon the hearts of the people.

Zwingli's labors at Einsiedeln had prepared him for a wider field, and this he was soon to enter. After three years here he was called to the office of preacher in the cathedral at Zurich. This was then the most important town of the Swiss confederacy, and the influence exerted here would be widely felt. The ecclesiastics by whose invitation he came to Zurich were, however, desirous of preventing any innovations, and they accordingly proceeded to instruct him as to his duties.

"You will make every exertion," they said, "to collect the revenues of the chapter, without overlooking the least. You will exhort the faithful, both from the pulpit and in the confessional, to pay all tithes and dues, and to show by their offerings their affection to the church. You will be diligent in increasing the income arising from the sick, from masses, and in general from every ecclesiastical ordinance." "As for the administration of the sacraments, the preaching, and the care of the flock," added his instructors, "these are also the duties of the chaplain. But for these you may employ a substitute, and particularly in preaching. You should administer the sacraments to none but persons of note, and only when called upon; you are forbidden to do so without distinction of persons." —*Ibid.*, b. 8, ch. 6.

Zwingli listened in silence to this charge, and in reply, after expressing his gratitude for the honor of a call to this important station, he proceeded to explain the course which he proposed to adopt. "The life of Christ," he said, "has been too long hidden from the people. I shall preach upon the whole of the Gospel of St. Matthew, ... drawing solely from the fountains of Scripture, sounding its depths, comparing one passage with another, and seeking for understanding by constant and earnest prayer. It is to God's glory, to the praise of His only Son, to the real salvation of souls, and to their edification in the true faith, that I shall consecrate my ministry." —*Ibid.*, b. 8, ch. 6. Though some of the ecclesiastics disapproved his plan, and endeavored to dissuade him from it, Zwingli remained steadfast. He declared that he was about to introduce no new method, but the old method employed by the church in earlier and purer times.

Already an interest had been awakened in the truths he taught; and the people flocked in great numbers to listen to his preaching. Many who had long since ceased to attend service were among his hearers. He began his ministry by opening the Gospels and reading and explaining to his hearers the inspired narrative of the life, teachings, and death of Christ. Here, as at Einsiedeln, he presented the word of God as the only infallible authority and the death of Christ as the only complete sacrifice. "It is to Christ," he said, "that I desire to lead you—to Christ, the true source of salvation." —*Ibid.*, b. 8, ch. 6. Around the preacher crowded the people of all classes, from statesmen and scholars to the artisan and the peasant. With deep interest they listened to his words. He not only proclaimed the offer of a free salvation, but fearlessly rebuked the evils and corruptions of the times. Many returned from the cathedral praising God. "This man," they said, "is a preacher of the truth. He will be our Moses, to lead us forth from this Egyptian darkness." —*Ibid.*, b. 8, ch. 6.

But though at first his labors were received with great enthusiasm, after a time opposition arose. The monks set themselves to hinder his work and condemn his teachings. Many assailed him with gibes and sneers; others resorted to insolence and threats. But Zwingli bore all with patience, saying: "If we desire to gain over the wicked to Jesus Christ, we must shut our eyes against many things." —*Ibid.*, b. 8, ch. 6.

About this time a new agency came in to advance the work of reform. One Lucian was sent to Zurich with some of Luther's writings, by a friend of the reformed faith at Basel, who suggested that the sale of these books might be a powerful means of scattering the light. "Ascertain," he wrote to Zwingli, "whether this man possesses sufficient prudence and skill; if so, let him carry from city to city, from town to town, from village to village, and even from house to house, among the Swiss, the works of Luther, and especially his exposition of the Lord's Prayer written for the laity. The more they are known, the more purchasers they will find." —*Ibid.*, b. 8, ch. 6. Thus the light found entrance.

At the time when God is preparing to break the shackles of ignorance and superstition, then it is that Satan works with greatest power to enshroud men in darkness and to bind their fetters still more firmly. As men were rising up in different lands to present to the people forgiveness and justification through the blood of Christ, Rome proceeded with renewed energy to open her market throughout Christendom, offering pardon for money.

Every sin had its price, and men were granted free license for crime if the treasury of the church was kept well filled. Thus the two movements advanced,—one offering forgiveness of sin for money, the other forgiveness through Christ,—Rome licensing sin and making it her source of revenue; the Reformers condemning sin and pointing to Christ as the propitiation and deliverer.

In Germany the sale of indulgences had been committed to the Dominican friars and was conducted by the infamous Tetzel. In Switzerland the traffic was put into the hands of the Franciscans, under the control of Samson, an Italian monk. Samson had already done good service to the church, having secured immense sums from Germany and Switzerland to fill the papal treasury. Now he traversed Switzerland, attracting great crowds, despoiling the poor peasants of their scanty earnings, and exacting rich gifts from the wealthy classes. But the influence of the reform already made itself felt in curtailing, though it could not stop, the traffic. Zwingli was still at Einsiedeln when Samson, soon after entering Switzerland, arrived with his wares at a neighboring town. Being apprised of his mission, the Reformer immediately set out to oppose him. The two did not meet, but such was Zwingli's success in exposing the friar's pretensions that he was obliged to leave for other quarters.

At Zurich, Zwingli preached zealously against the pardonmongers; and when Samson approached the place, he was met by a messenger from the council with an intimation that he was expected to pass on. He finally secured an entrance by stratagem, but was sent away without the sale of a single pardon, and he soon after left Switzerland.

A strong impetus was given to the reform by the appearance of the plague, or Great Death, which swept over Switzerland in the year 1519. As men were thus brought face to face with the destroyer, many were led to feel how vain and worthless were the pardons which they had so lately purchased; and they longed for a surer foundation for their faith. Zwingli at Zurich was smitten down; he was brought so low that all hope of his recovery was relinquished, and the report was widely circulated that he was dead. In that trying hour his hope and courage were unshaken. He looked in faith to the cross of Calvary, trusting in the all-sufficient propitiation for sin. When he came back from the gates of death, it was to preach the gospel with greater fervor than ever before; and his words exerted an unwonted power. The people welcomed with joy their beloved pastor, returned to them from the brink of the grave. They themselves had come from attending upon the sick and the dying, and they felt, as never before, the value of the gospel.

Zwingli had arrived at a clearer understanding of its truths, and had more fully experienced in himself its renewing power. The fall of man and the plan of redemption were the subjects upon which he dwelt. "In Adam," he said, "we are all dead, sunk in corruption and condemnation." —Wylie, b. 8, ch. 9. "Christ … has purchased for us a never-ending redemption. … His passion is … an eternal sacrifice, and everlastingly effectual to heal; it satisfies the divine justice forever in behalf of all those who rely upon it with firm and unshaken faith." Yet he clearly taught that men are not, because of the grace of Christ, free to continue in sin. "Wherever there is faith in God, there God is; and wherever God abideth, there a zeal exists urging and impelling men to good works." —D'Aubigne, b. 8, ch. 9.

Such was the interest in Zwingli's preaching that the cathedral was filled to overflowing with the crowds that came to listen to him. Little by little, as they could bear it, he opened the truth to his hearers. He was careful not to introduce, at first, points which would startle them and create prejudice. His work was to win their hearts to the teachings of Christ, to soften them by His love, and keep before them His example; and as they should receive the principles of the gospel, their superstitious beliefs and practices would inevitably be overthrown.

Step by step the Reformation advanced in Zurich. In alarm its enemies aroused to active opposition. One year before, the monk of Wittenberg had uttered his No to the pope and the emperor at Worms, and now everything seemed to indicate a similar withstanding of the papal claims at Zurich. Repeated attacks were made upon Zwingli. In the papal cantons, from time to time, disciples of the gospel were brought to the stake, but this was not enough; the teacher of heresy must be silenced. Accordingly the bishop of Constance dispatched three deputies to the Council of Zurich, accusing Zwingli of teaching the people to transgress the laws of the church, thus endangering the peace and good order of society. If the authority of the church were to be set aside, he urged, universal anarchy would result. Zwingli replied that he had been for four years teaching the gospel in Zurich, "which was more quiet and peaceful than any other town in the confederacy." "Is not, then," he said, "Christianity the best safeguard of the general security?" —Wylie, b. 8, ch. 11.

The deputies had admonished the councilors to continue in the church, out of which, they declared, there was no salvation. Zwingli responded: "Let not this accusation move you. The foundation of the church is the same Rock, the same Christ, that gave Peter his name because he confessed Him faithfully. In every nation whosoever believes with all his heart in the Lord Jesus is accepted of God. Here, truly, is the church, out of which no one can be saved." —D'Aubigne, London ed., b. 8, ch. 11. As a result of the conference, one of the bishop's deputies accepted the reformed faith.

The council declined to take action against Zwingli, and Rome prepared for a fresh attack. The Reformer, when apprised of the plots of his enemies, exclaimed: "Let them come on; I fear them as the beetling cliff fears the waves that thunder at its feet." —Wylie, b. 8, ch. 11. The efforts of the ecclesiastics only furthered the cause which they sought to overthrow. The truth continued to spread. In Germany its adherents, cast down by Luther's disappearance, took heart again, as they saw the progress of the gospel in Switzerland.

As the Reformation became established in Zurich, its fruits were more fully seen in the suppression of vice and the promotion of order and harmony. "Peace has her habitation in our town," wrote Zwingli; "no quarrel, no hypocrisy, no envy, no strife. Whence can such union come but from the Lord, and our doctrine, which fills us with the fruits of peace and piety?" —*Ibid.*, b. 8, ch. 15.

The victories gained by the Reformation stirred the Romanists to still more determined efforts for its overthrow. Seeing how little had been accomplished by persecution in suppressing Luther's work in Germany, they decided to meet the reform with its own weapons. They would hold a disputation with Zwingli, and having the arrangement of matters, they would make sure of victory by choosing, themselves, not only the place of the combat, but the judges that should decide between the disputants. And if they could once get Zwingli into their power, they would take care that he did not escape them. The leader silenced, the movement could speedily be crushed. This purpose, however, was carefully concealed.

The disputation was appointed to be held at Baden; but Zwingli was not present. The Council of Zurich, suspecting the designs of the papists, and warned by the burning piles kindled in the papal cantons for confessors of the gospel, forbade their pastor to expose himself to this peril. At Zurich he was ready to meet all the partisans that Rome might send; but to go to Baden, where the blood of martyrs for the truth had just been shed, was to go to certain death. Oecolampadius and Haller were chosen to represent the Reformers, while the famous Dr. Eck, supported by a host of learned doctors and prelates, was the champion of Rome.

Though Zwingli was not present at the conference, his influence was felt. The secretaries were all chosen by the papists, and others were forbidden to take notes, on pain of death. Notwithstanding this, Zwingli received daily a faithful account of what was said at Baden. A student in attendance at the disputation made a record each evening of the arguments that day presented. These papers two other students undertook to deliver, with the daily letters of Oecolampadius, to Zwingli at Zurich. The Reformer answered, giving counsel and suggestions. His letters were written by night, and the students returned with them to Baden in the morning. To elude the vigilance of the guard stationed at the city gates, these messengers brought baskets of poultry on their heads, and they were permitted to pass without hindrance.

Thus Zwingli maintained the battle with his wily antagonists. He "has labored more," said Myconius, "by his meditations, his sleepless nights, and the advice which he transmitted to Baden, than he would have done by discussing in person in the midst of his enemies." —D'Aubigne, b. 11, ch. 13.

The Romanists, flushed with anticipated triumph, had come to Baden attired in their richest robes and glittering with jewels. They fared luxuriously, their tables spread with the most costly delicacies and the choicest wines. The burden of their ecclesiastical duties was lightened by gaiety and reveling. In marked contrast appeared the Reformers, who were looked upon by the people as little better than a company of beggars, and whose frugal fare kept them but short time at table. Oecolampadius's landlord, taking occasion to watch him in his room, found him always engaged in study or at prayer, and greatly wondering, reported that the heretic was at least "very pious."

At the conference, "Eck haughtily ascended a pulpit splendidly decorated, while the humble Oecolampadius, meanly clothed, was forced to take his seat in front of his opponent on a rudely carved stool." —*Ibid.*, b. 11, ch. 13. Eck's stentorian voice and unbounded assurance never failed him. His zeal was stimulated by the hope of gold as well as fame; for the defender of the faith was to be rewarded by a handsome fee. When better arguments failed, he had resort to insults, and even to oaths.

Oecolampadius, modest and self-distrustful, had shrunk from the combat, and he entered upon it with the solemn avowal: "I acknowledge no other standard of judgment than the word of God." —*Ibid.*, b. 11, ch. 13. Though gentle and courteous in demeanor, he proved himself able and unflinching. While the Romanists, according to their wont, appealed for authority to the customs of the church, the Reformer adhered steadfastly to the Holy Scriptures. "Custom," he said, "has no force in our Switzerland, unless it be according to the constitution; now, in matters of faith, the Bible is our constitution." —*Ibid.*, b. 11, ch. 13.

The contrast between the two disputants was not without effect. The calm, clear reasoning of the Reformer, so gently and modestly presented, appealed to minds that turned in disgust from Eck's boastful and boisterous assumptions.

The discussion continued eighteen days. At its close the papists with great confidence claimed the victory. Most of the deputies sided with Rome, and the Diet pronounced the Reformers vanquished and declared that they, together with Zwingli, their leader, were cut off from the church. But the fruits of the conference revealed on which side the advantage lay. The contest resulted in a strong impetus to the Protestant cause, and it was not long afterward that the important cities of Bern and Basel declared for the Reformation.

Seven

—Progress of Reform in Germany—

Luther's mysterious disappearance excited consternation throughout all Germany. Inquiries concerning him were heard everywhere. The wildest rumors were circulated, and many believed that he had been murdered. There was great lamentation, not only by his avowed friends, but by thousands who had not openly taken their stand with the Reformation. Many bound themselves by a solemn oath to avenge his death.

The Romish leaders saw with terror to what a pitch had risen the feeling against them. Though at first exultant at the supposed death of Luther, they soon desired to hide from the wrath of the people. His enemies had not been so troubled by his most daring acts while among them as they were at his removal. Those who in their rage had sought to destroy the bold Reformer were filled with fear now that he had become a helpless captive. "The only remaining way of saving ourselves," said one, "is to light torches, and hunt for Luther through the whole world, to restore him to the nation that is calling for him." —D'Aubigne, b. 9, ch. 1. The edict of the emperor seemed to fall powerless. The papal legates were filled with indignation as they saw that it commanded far less attention than did the fate of Luther.

The tidings that he was safe, though a prisoner, calmed the fears of the people, while it still further aroused their enthusiasm in his favor. His writings were read with greater eagerness than ever before. Increasing numbers joined the cause of the heroic man who had, at such fearful odds, defended the word of God. The Reformation was constantly gaining in strength. The seed which Luther had sown sprang up everywhere. His absence accomplished a work which his presence would have failed to do. Other laborers felt a new responsibility, now that their great leader was removed. With new faith and earnestness they pressed forward to do all in their power, that the work so nobly begun might not be hindered.

But Satan was not idle. He now attempted what he has attempted in every other reformatory movement—to deceive and destroy the people by palming off upon them a counterfeit in place of the true work. As there were false christs in the first century of the Christian church, so there arose false prophets in the sixteenth century.

A few men, deeply affected by the excitement in the religious world, imagined themselves to have received special revelations from Heaven, and claimed to have been divinely commissioned to carry forward to its completion the Reformation which, they declared, had been but feebly begun by Luther. In truth, they were undoing the very work which he had accomplished. They rejected the great principle which was the very foundation of the Reformation—that the word of God is the all-sufficient rule of faith and practice; and for that unerring guide they substituted the changeable, uncertain standard of their own feelings and impressions. By this act of setting aside the great detector of error and falsehood the way was opened for Satan to control minds as best pleased himself.

One of these prophets claimed to have been instructed by the angel Gabriel. A student who united with him forsook his studies, declaring that he had been endowed by God Himself with wisdom to expound His word. Others who were naturally inclined to fanaticism united with them. The proceedings of these enthusiasts created no little excitement. The preaching of Luther had aroused the people everywhere to feel the necessity of reform, and now some really honest persons were misled by the pretensions of the new prophets.

The leaders of the movement proceeded to Wittenberg and urged their claims upon Melanchthon and his colaborers. Said they: "We are sent by God to instruct the people. We have held familiar conversations with the Lord; we know what will happen; in a word, we are apostles and prophets, and appeal to Dr. Luther." —*Ibid.,* b. 9, ch. 7.

The Reformers were astonished and perplexed. This was such an element as they had never before encountered, and they knew not what course to pursue. Said Melanchthon: "There are indeed extraordinary spirits in these men; but what spirits? ... On the one hand, let us beware of quenching the Spirit of God, and on the other, of being led astray by the spirit of Satan." —*Ibid.,* b. 9, ch. 7.

The fruit of the new teaching soon became apparent. The people were led to neglect the Bible or to cast it wholly aside. The schools were thrown into confusion. Students, spurning all restraint, abandoned their studies and withdrew from the university. The men who thought themselves competent to revive and control the work of the Reformation succeeded only in bringing it to the verge of ruin. The Romanists now regained their confidence and exclaimed exultingly: "One last struggle, and all will be ours." —*Ibid.,* b. 9, ch. 7.

Luther at the Wartburg, hearing of what had occurred, said with deep concern: "I always expected that Satan would send us this plague." —*Ibid.,* b. 9, ch. 7. He perceived the true character of those pretended prophets and saw the danger that threatened the cause of truth. The opposition of the pope and the emperor had not caused him so great perplexity and distress as he now experienced. From the professed friends of the Reformation had risen its worst enemies. The very truths which had brought him so great joy and consolation were being employed to stir up strife and create confusion in the church.

In the work of reform, Luther had been urged forward by the Spirit of God, and had been carried beyond himself. He had not purposed to take such positions as he did, or to make so radical changes. He had been but the instrument in the hand of Infinite Power. Yet he often trembled for the result of his work. He had once said: "If I knew that my doctrine injured one man, one single man, however lowly and obscure,—which it cannot, for it is the gospel itself,—I would rather die ten times than not retract it." —*Ibid.*, b. 9, ch. 7.

And now Wittenberg itself, the very center of the Reformation, was fast falling under the power of fanaticism and lawlessness. This terrible condition had not resulted from the teachings of Luther; but throughout Germany his enemies were charging it upon him. In bitterness of soul he sometimes asked: "Can such, then, be the end of this great work of the Reformation?" —*Ibid.*, b. 9, ch. 7. Again, as he wrestled with God in prayer, peace flowed into his heart. "The work is not mine, but Thine own," he said; "Thou wilt not suffer it to be corrupted by superstition or fanaticism." But the thought of remaining longer from the conflict in such a crisis, became insupportable. He determined to return to Wittenberg.

Without delay he set out on his perilous journey. He was under the ban of the empire. Enemies were at liberty to take his life; friends were forbidden to aid or shelter him. The imperial government was adopting the most stringent measures against his adherents. But he saw that the work of the gospel was imperiled, and in the name of the Lord he went out fearlessly to battle for the truth.

In a letter to the elector, after stating his purpose to leave the Wartburg, Luther said: "Be it known to your highness that I am going to Wittenberg under a protection far higher than that of princes and electors. I think not of soliciting your highness's support, and far from desiring your protection, I would rather protect you myself. If I knew that your highness could or would protect me, I would not go to Wittenberg at all. There is no sword that can further this cause. God alone must do everything, without the help or concurrence of man. He who has the greatest faith is he who is most able to protect." —*Ibid.*, b. 9, ch. 8.

In a second letter, written on the way to Wittenberg, Luther added: "I am ready to incur the displeasure of your highness and the anger of the whole world. Are not the Wittenbergers my sheep? Has not God entrusted them to me? And ought I not, if necessary, to expose myself to death for their sakes? Besides, I fear to see a terrible outbreak in Germany, by which God will punish our nation." —*Ibid.*, b. 9, ch. 7.

With great caution and humility, yet with decision and firmness, he entered upon his work. "By the word," said he, "must we overthrow and destroy what has been set up by violence. I will not make use of force against the superstitious and unbelieving. ... No one must be constrained. Liberty is the very essence of faith." —*Ibid.,* b. 9, ch. 8.

It was soon noised through Wittenberg that Luther had returned and that he was to preach. The people flocked from all directions, and the church was filled to overflowing. Ascending the pulpit, he with great wisdom and gentleness instructed, exhorted, and reproved. Touching the course of some who had resorted to violent measures in abolishing the mass, he said:

"The mass is a bad thing; God is opposed to it; it ought to be abolished; and I would that throughout the whole world it were replaced by the supper of the gospel. But let no one be torn from it by force. We must leave the matter in God's hands. His word must act, and not we. And why so? you will ask. Because I do not hold men's hearts in my hand, as the potter holds the clay. We have a right to speak: we have *not* the right to act. Let us preach; the rest belongs unto God. Were I to employ force, what should I gain? Grimace, formality, apings, human ordinances, and hypocrisy. ... But there would be no sincerity of heart, nor faith, nor charity. Where these three are wanting, all is wanting, and I would not give a pear stalk for such a result. ... God does more by His word alone than you and I and all the world by our united strength. God lays hold upon the heart; and when the heart is taken, all is won. ...

"I will preach, discuss, and write; but I will constrain none, for faith is a voluntary act. See what I have done. I stood up against the pope, indulgences, and papists, but without violence or tumult. I put forward God's word; I preached and wrote—this was all I did. And yet while I was asleep, ... the word that I had preached overthrew popery, so that neither prince nor emperor has done it so much harm. And yet I did nothing; the word alone did all. If I had wished to appeal to force, the whole of Germany would perhaps have been deluged with blood. But what would have been the result? Ruin and desolation both to body and soul. I therefore kept quiet, and left the word to run through the world alone." —*Ibid.,* b. 9, ch. 8.

Day after day, for a whole week, Luther continued to preach to eager crowds. The word of God broke the spell of fanatical excitement. The power of the gospel brought back the misguided people into the way of truth.

Luther had no desire to encounter the fanatics whose course had been productive of so great evil. He knew them to be men of unsound judgment and undisciplined passions, who, while claiming to be specially illuminated from heaven, would not endure the slightest contradiction or even the kindest reproof or counsel. Arrogating to themselves supreme authority, they required everyone, without a question, to acknowledge their claims. But, as they demanded an interview with him, he consented to meet them; and so successfully did he expose their pretensions that the impostors at once departed from Wittenberg.

The fanaticism was checked for a time; but several years later it broke out with greater violence and more terrible results. Said Luther, concerning the leaders in this movement: "To them the Holy Scriptures were but a dead letter, and they all began to cry, 'The Spirit! the Spirit!' But most assuredly I will not follow where their spirit leads them. May God of His mercy preserve me from a church in which there are none but saints. I desire to dwell with the humble, the feeble, the sick, who know and feel their sins, and who groan and cry continually to God from the bottom of their hearts to obtain His consolation and support." —*Ibid.*, b. 10, ch. 10.

Thomas Münzer, the most active of the fanatics, was a man of considerable ability, which, rightly directed, would have enabled him to do good; but he had not learned the first principles of true religion. "He was possessed with a desire of reforming the world, and forgot, as all enthusiasts do, that the reformation should begin with himself." —*Ibid.*, b. 9, ch. 8. He was ambitious to obtain position and influence, and was unwilling to be second, even to Luther. He declared that the Reformers, in substituting the authority of Scripture for that of the pope, were only establishing a different form of popery. He himself, he claimed, had been divinely commissioned to introduce the true reform. "He who possesses this spirit," said Münzer, "possesses the true faith, although he should never see the Scriptures in his life." —*Ibid.*, b. 10, ch. 10.

The fanatical teachers gave themselves up to be governed by impressions, regarding every thought and impulse as the voice of God; consequently they went to great extremes. Some even burned their Bibles, exclaiming: "The letter killeth, but the Spirit giveth life." Münzer's teaching appealed to men's desire for the marvelous, while it gratified their pride by virtually placing human ideas and opinions above the word of God. His doctrines were received by thousands. He soon denounced all order in public worship, and declared that to obey princes was to attempt to serve both God and Belial.

The minds of the people, already beginning to throw off the yoke of the papacy, were also becoming impatient under the restraints of civil authority. Münzer's revolutionary teachings, claiming divine sanction, led them to break away from all control and give the rein to their prejudices and passions. The most terrible scenes of sedition and strife followed, and the fields of Germany were drenched with blood.

The agony of soul which Luther had so long before experienced at Erfurt now pressed upon him with redoubled power as he saw the results of fanaticism charged upon the Reformation. The papist princes declared—and many were ready to credit the statement—that the rebellion was the legitimate fruit of Luther's doctrines. Although this charge was without the slightest foundation, it could not but cause the Reformer great distress. That the cause of truth should be thus disgraced by being ranked with the basest fanaticism, seemed more than he could endure. On the other hand, the leaders in the revolt hated

Luther because he had not only opposed their doctrines and denied their claims to divine inspiration, but had pronounced them rebels against the civil authority. In retaliation they denounced him as a base pretender. He seemed to have brought upon himself the enmity of both princes and people.

The Romanists exulted, expecting to witness the speedy downfall of the Reformation; and they blamed Luther, even for the errors which he had been most earnestly endeavoring to correct. The fanatical party, by falsely claiming to have been treated with great injustice, succeeded in gaining the sympathies of a large class of the people, and, as is often the case with those who take the wrong side, they came to be regarded as martyrs. Thus the ones who were exerting every energy in opposition to the Reformation were pitied and lauded as the victims of cruelty and oppression. This was the work of Satan, prompted by the same spirit of rebellion which was first manifested in heaven.

Satan is constantly seeking to deceive men and lead them to call sin righteousness, and righteousness sin. How successful has been his work! How often censure and reproach are cast upon God's faithful servants because they will stand fearlessly in defense of the truth! Men who are but agents of Satan are praised and flattered, and even looked upon as martyrs, while those who should be respected and sustained for their fidelity to God, are left to stand alone, under suspicion and distrust.

Counterfeit holiness, spurious sanctification, is still doing its work of deception. Under various forms it exhibits the same spirit as in the days of Luther, diverting minds from the Scriptures and leading men to follow their own feelings and impressions rather than to yield obedience to the law of God. This is one of Satan's most successful devices to cast reproach upon purity and truth.

Fearlessly did Luther defend the gospel from the attacks which came from every quarter. The word of God proved itself a weapon mighty in every conflict. With that word he warred against the usurped authority of the pope, and the rationalistic philosophy of the schoolmen, while he stood firm as a rock against the fanaticism that sought to ally itself with the Reformation.

Each of these opposing elements was in its own way setting aside the Holy Scriptures and exalting human wisdom as the source of religious truth and knowledge. Rationalism idolizes reason and makes this the criterion for religion. Romanism, claiming for her sovereign pontiff an inspiration descended in unbroken line from the apostles, and unchangeable through all time, gives ample opportunity for every species of extravagance and corruption to be concealed under the sanctity of the apostolic commission. The inspiration claimed by Münzer and his associates proceeded from no higher source than the vagaries of the imagination, and its influence was subversive of all authority, human or divine. True Christianity receives the word of God as the great treasure house of inspired truth and the test of all inspiration.

Upon his return from the Wartburg, Luther completed his translation of the New Testament, and the gospel was soon after given to the people of Germany in their own language. This translation was received with great joy by all who loved the truth; but it was scornfully rejected by those who chose human traditions and the commandments of men.

The priests were alarmed at the thought that the common people would now be able to discuss with them the precepts of God's word, and that their own ignorance would thus be exposed. The weapons of their carnal reasoning were powerless against the sword of the Spirit. Rome summoned all her authority to prevent the circulation of the Scriptures; but decrees, anathemas, and tortures were alike in vain. The more she condemned and prohibited the Bible, the greater was the anxiety of the people to know what it really taught. All who could read were eager to study the word of God for themselves. They carried it about with them, and read and reread, and could not be satisfied until they had committed large portions to memory. Seeing the favor with which the New Testament was received, Luther immediately began the translation of the Old, and published it in parts as fast as completed.

Luther's writings were welcomed alike in city and in hamlet. "What Luther and his friends composed, others circulated. Monks, convinced of the unlawfulness of monastic obligations, desirous of exchanging a long life of slothfulness for one of active exertion, but too ignorant to proclaim the word of God, traveled through the provinces, visiting hamlets and cottages, where they sold the books of Luther and his friends. Germany soon swarmed with these bold colporteurs." —*Ibid.,* b. 9, ch. 11.

These writings were studied with deep interest by rich and poor, the learned and the ignorant. At night the teachers of the village schools read them aloud to little groups gathered at the fireside. With every effort some souls would be convicted of the truth and, receiving the word with gladness, would in their turn tell the good news to others.

The words of Inspiration were verified: "The entrance of Thy words giveth light; it giveth understanding unto the simple." Psalm 119:130. The study of the Scriptures was working a mighty change in the minds and hearts of the people. The papal rule had placed upon its subjects an iron yoke which held them in ignorance and degradation. A superstitious observance of forms had been scrupulously maintained; but in all their service the heart and intellect had had little part. The preaching of Luther, setting forth the plain truths of God's word, and then the word itself, placed in the hands of the common people, had aroused their dormant powers, not only purifying and ennobling the spiritual nature, but imparting new strength and vigor to the intellect.

Persons of all ranks were to be seen with the Bible in their hands, defending the doctrines of the Reformation. The papists who had left the study of the Scriptures to the priests and monks now called upon them to come forward and refute the new teachings. But, ignorant alike of the Scriptures and of the power of God, priests and friars were totally defeated by those whom they had denounced as unlearned and heretical. "Unhappily," said a Catholic writer, "Luther had persuaded his followers to put no faith in any other oracle than the Holy Scriptures." —D'Aubigne, b. 9, ch. 11. Crowds would gather to hear the truth advocated by men of little education, and even discussed by them with learned and eloquent theologians. The shameful ignorance of these great men was made apparent as their arguments were met by the simple teachings of God's word. Laborers, soldiers, women, and even children, were better acquainted with the Bible teachings than were the priests and learned doctors.

The contrast between the disciples of the gospel and the upholders of popish superstition was no less manifest in the ranks of scholars than among the common people. "Opposed to the old champions of the hierarchy, who had neglected the study of languages and the cultivation of literature, ... were generous-minded youth, devoted to study, investigating Scripture, and familiarizing themselves with the masterpieces of antiquity. Possessing an active mind, an elevated soul, and intrepid heart, these young men soon acquired such knowledge that for a long period none could compete with them. ... Accordingly, when these youthful defenders of the Reformation met the Romish doctors in any assembly, they attacked them with such ease and confidence that these ignorant men hesitated, became embarrassed, and fell into a contempt merited in the eyes of all." —*Ibid.,* b. 9, ch. 11.

As the Romish clergy saw their congregations diminishing, they invoked the aid of the magistrates, and by every means in their power endeavored to bring back their hearers. But the people had found in the new teachings that which supplied the wants of their souls, and they turned away from those who had so long fed them with the worthless husks of superstitious rites and human traditions.

When persecution was kindled against the teachers of the truth, they gave heed to the words of Christ: "When they persecute you in this city, flee ye into another." Matthew 10:23. The light penetrated everywhere. The fugitives would find somewhere a hospitable door opened to them, and there abiding, they would preach Christ, sometimes in the church, or, if denied that privilege, in private houses or in the open air. Wherever they could obtain a hearing was a consecrated temple. The truth, proclaimed with such energy and assurance, spread with irresistible power.

In vain both ecclesiastical and civil authorities were invoked to crush the heresy. In vain they resorted to imprisonment, torture, fire, and sword. Thousands of believers sealed their faith with their blood, and yet the work went on. Persecution served only to extend the truth, and the fanaticism which Satan endeavored to unite with it resulted in making more clear the contrast between the work of Satan and the work of God.

Eight

—Later English Reformers—

While Luther was opening a closed Bible to the people of Germany, Tyndale was impelled by the Spirit of God to do the same for England Wycliffe's Bible had been translated from the Latin text, which contained many errors. It had never been printed, and the cost of manuscript copies was so great that few but wealthy men or nobles could procure it; and, furthermore, being strictly proscribed by the church, it had had a comparatively narrow circulation. In 1516, a year before the appearance of Luther's theses, Erasmus had published his Greek and Latin version of the New Testament. Now for the first time the word of God was printed in the original tongue. In this work many errors of former versions were corrected, and the sense was more clearly rendered. It led many among the educated classes to a better knowledge of the truth, and gave a new impetus to the work of reform. But the common people were still, to a great extent, debarred from God's word. Tyndale was to complete the work of Wycliffe in giving the Bible to his countrymen.

A diligent student and an earnest seeker for truth, he had received the gospel from the Greek Testament of Erasmus. He fearlessly preached his convictions, urging that all doctrines be tested by the Scriptures. To the papist claim that the church had given the Bible, and the church alone could explain it, Tyndale responded: "Do you know who taught the eagles to find their prey? Well, that same God teaches His hungry children to find their Father in His word. Far from having given us the Scriptures, it is you who have hidden them from us; it is you who burn those who teach them, and if you could, you would burn the Scriptures themselves." —D'Aubigne, *History of the Reformation of the Sixteenth Century*, b. 18, ch. 4.

Tyndale's preaching excited great interest; many accepted the truth. But the priests were on the alert, and no sooner had he left the field than they by their threats and misrepresentations endeavored to destroy his work. Too often they succeeded. "What is to be done?" he exclaimed. "While I am sowing in one place, the enemy ravages the field I have just left. I cannot be everywhere. Oh! if Christians possessed the Holy Scriptures in their own tongue, they could of themselves withstand these sophists. Without the Bible it is impossible to establish the laity in the truth." —*Ibid.*, b. 18, ch. 4.

A new purpose now took possession of his mind. "It was in the language of Israel," said he, "that the psalms were sung in the temple of Jehovah; and shall not the gospel speak the language of England among us? ... Ought the church to have less light at noonday than at the dawn? ... Christians must read the New Testament in their mother tongue." The doctors and teachers of the church disagreed among themselves. Only by the Bible could men arrive at the truth. "One holdeth this doctor, another that. ... Now each of these authors contradicts the other. How then can we distinguish him who says right from him who says wrong? ... How? ... Verily by God's word." —*Ibid.,* b. 18, ch. 4.

It was not long after that a learned Catholic doctor, engaging in controversy with him, exclaimed: "We were better to be without God's laws than the pope's." Tyndale replied: "I defy the pope and all his laws; and if God spare my life, ere many years I will cause a boy that driveth the plow to know more of the Scripture than you do." —Anderson, *Annals of the English Bible,* page 19.

The purpose which he had begun to cherish, of giving to the people the New Testament Scriptures in their own language, was now confirmed, and he immediately applied himself to the work. Driven from his home by persecution, he went to London, and there for a time pursued his labors undisturbed. But again the violence of the papists forced him to flee. All England seemed closed against him, and he resolved to seek shelter in Germany. Here he began the printing of the English New Testament. Twice the work was stopped; but when forbidden to print in one city, he went to another. At last he made his way to Worms, where, a few years before, Luther had defended the gospel before the Diet. In that ancient city were many friends of the Reformation, and Tyndale there prosecuted his work without further hindrance. Three thousand copies of the New Testament were soon finished, and another edition followed in the same year.

With great earnestness and perseverance he continued his labors. Notwithstanding the English authorities had guarded their ports with the strictest vigilance, the word of God was in various ways secretly conveyed to London and thence circulated throughout the country. The papists attempted to suppress the truth, but in vain. The bishop of Durham at one time bought of a bookseller who was a friend of Tyndale his whole stock of Bibles, for the purpose of destroying them, supposing that this would greatly hinder the work. But, on the contrary, the money thus furnished, purchased material for a new and better edition, which, but for this, could not have been published. When Tyndale was afterward made a prisoner, his liberty was offered him on condition that he would reveal the names of those who had helped him meet the expense of printing his Bibles. He replied that the bishop of Durham had done more than any other person; for by paying a large price for the books left on hand, he had enabled him to go on with good courage.

Tyndale was betrayed into the hands of his enemies, and at one time suffered imprisonment for many months. He finally witnessed for his faith by a martyr's death; but the weapons which he prepared have enabled other soldiers to do battle through all the centuries even to our time.

Latimer maintained from the pulpit that the Bible ought to be read in the language of the people. The Author of Holy Scripture, said he, "is God Himself;" and this Scripture partakes of the might and eternity of its Author. "There is no king, emperor, magistrate, and ruler ... but are bound to obey ... His holy word." "Let us not take any bywalks, but let God's word direct us: let us not walk after ... our forefathers, nor seek not what they did, but what they should have done." —Hugh Latimer, "First Sermon Preached Before King Edward VI."

Barnes and Frith, the faithful friends of Tyndale, arose to defend the truth. The Ridleys and Cranmer followed. These leaders in the English Reformation were men of learning, and most of them had been highly esteemed for zeal or piety in the Romish communion. Their opposition to the papacy was the result of their knowledge of the errors of the "holy see." Their acquaintance with the mysteries of Babylon gave greater power to their testimonies against her.

"Now I would ask a strange question," said Latimer. "Who is the most diligent bishop and prelate in all England? ... I see you listening and hearkening that I should name him. ... I will tell you: it is the devil. ... He is never out of his diocese; call for him when you will, he is ever at home; ... he is ever at his plow. ... Ye shall never find him idle, I warrant you. ... Where the devil is resident, ... there away with books, and up with candles; away with Bibles, and up with beads; away with the light of the gospel, and up with the light of candles, yea, at noondays; ... down with Christ's cross, up with purgatory pickpurse; ... away with clothing the naked, the poor, and impotent, up with decking of images and gay garnishing of stocks and stones; up with man's traditions and his laws, down with God's traditions and His most holy word. ... O that our prelates would be as diligent to sow the corn of good doctrine, as Satan is to sow cockle and darnel!" —*Ibid.,* "Sermon of the Plough."

The grand principle maintained by these Reformers—the same that had been held by the Waldenses, by Wycliffe, by John Huss, by Luther, Zwingli, and those who united with them—was the infallible authority of the Holy Scriptures as a rule of faith and practice. They denied the right of popes, councils, Fathers, and kings, to control the conscience in matters of religion. The Bible was their authority, and by its teaching they tested all doctrines and all claims. Faith in God and His word sustained these holy men as they yielded up their lives at the stake. "Be of good comfort," exclaimed Latimer to his fellow martyr as the flames were about to silence their voices, "we shall this day light such a candle, by God's grace, in England, as I trust shall never be put out." —*Works of Hugh Latimer,* vol. 1, p. xiii.

In Scotland the seeds of truth scattered by Columba and his colaborers had never been wholly destroyed. For hundreds of years after the churches of England submitted to Rome, those of Scotland maintained their freedom. In the twelfth century, however, popery became established here, and in no country did it exercise a more absolute sway. Nowhere was the darkness deeper. Still there came rays of light to pierce the gloom and give promise of the coming day. The Lollards, coming from England with the Bible and the teachings of Wycliffe, did much to preserve the knowledge of the gospel, and every century had its witnesses and martyrs.

With the opening of the Great Reformation came the writings of Luther, and then Tyndale's English New Testament. Unnoticed by the hierarchy, these messengers silently traversed the mountains and valleys, kindling into new life the torch of truth so nearly extinguished in Scotland, and undoing the work which Rome for four centuries of oppression had done.

Then the blood of martyrs gave fresh impetus to the movement. The papist leaders, suddenly awakening to the danger that threatened their cause, brought to the stake some of the noblest and most honored of the sons of Scotland. They did but erect a pulpit, from which the words of these dying witnesses were heard throughout the land, thrilling the souls of the people with an undying purpose to cast off the shackles of Rome.

Hamilton and Wishart, princely in character as in birth, with a long line of humbler disciples, yielded up their lives at the stake. But from the burning pile of Wishart there came one whom the flames were not to silence, one who under God was to strike the death knell of popery in Scotland.

John Knox had turned away from the traditions and mysticisms of the church, to feed upon the truths of God's word; and the teaching of Wishart had confirmed his determination to forsake the communion of Rome and join himself to the persecuted Reformers.

Urged by his companions to take the office of preacher, he shrank with trembling from its responsibility, and it was only after days of seclusion and painful conflict with himself that he consented. But having once accepted the position, he pressed forward with inflexible determination and undaunted courage as long as life continued. This truehearted Reformer feared not the face of man. The fires of martyrdom, blazing around him, served only to quicken his zeal to greater intensity. With the tyrant's ax held menacingly over his head, he stood his ground, striking sturdy blows on the right hand and on the left to demolish idolatry.

When brought face to face with the queen of Scotland, in whose presence the zeal of many a leader of the Protestants had abated, John Knox bore unswerving witness for the truth. He was not to be won by caresses; he quailed not before threats. The queen charged him with heresy. He had taught the people to receive a religion prohibited by the state, she declared, and had thus transgressed God's command enjoining subjects to obey their princes. Knox answered firmly:

"As right religion took neither original strength nor authority from worldly princes, but from the eternal God alone, so are not subjects bound to frame their religion according to the appetites of their princes. For oft it is that princes are the most ignorant of all others in God's true religion. ... If all the seed of Abraham had been of the religion of Pharaoh, whose subjects they long were, I pray you, madam, what religion would there have been in the world? Or if all men in the days of the apostles had been of the religion of the Roman emperors, what religion would there have been upon the face of the earth? ... And so, madam, ye may perceive that subjects are not bound to the religion of their princes, albeit they are commanded to give them obedience."

Said Mary: "Ye interpret the Scriptures in one manner, and they [the Roman Catholic teachers] interpret in another; whom shall I believe, and who shall be judge?"

"Ye shall believe God, that plainly speaketh in His word," answered the Reformer; "and farther than the word teaches you, ye neither shall believe the one nor the other. The word of God is plain in itself; and if there appear any obscurity in one place, the Holy Ghost, which is never contrary to Himself, explains the same more clearly in other places, so that there can remain no doubt but unto such as obstinately remain ignorant." —David Laing, *The Collected Works of John Knox*, vol. 2, pp. 281, 284.

Such were the truths that the fearless Reformer, at the peril of his life, spoke in the ear of royalty. With the same undaunted courage he kept to his purpose, praying and fighting the battles of the Lord, until Scotland was free from popery.

In England the establishment of Protestantism as the national religion diminished, but did not wholly stop, persecution. While many of the doctrines of Rome had been renounced, not a few of its forms were retained. The supremacy of the pope was rejected, but in his place the monarch was enthroned as the head of the church. In the service of the church there was still a wide departure from the purity and simplicity of the gospel. The great principle of religious liberty was not yet understood. Though the horrible cruelties which Rome employed against heresy were resorted to but rarely by Protestant rulers, yet the right of every man to worship God according to the dictates of his own conscience was not acknowledged. All were required to accept the doctrines and observe the forms of worship prescribed by the established church. Dissenters suffered persecution, to a greater or less extent, for hundreds of years.

In the seventeenth century thousands of pastors were expelled from their positions. The people were forbidden, on pain of heavy fines, imprisonment, and banishment, to attend any religious meetings except such as were sanctioned by the church. Those faithful souls who could not refrain from gathering to worship God were compelled to meet in dark alleys, in obscure garrets, and at some seasons in the woods at midnight. In the sheltering depths of the forest, a temple of God's own building, those scattered and persecuted children of the Lord assembled to pour out their souls in prayer and praise. But despite all their precautions, many suffered for their faith. The jails were crowded. Families were broken up. Many were banished to foreign lands. Yet God was with His people, and persecution could not prevail to silence their testimony. Many were driven across the ocean to America and here laid the foundations of civil and religious liberty which have been the bulwark and glory of this country.

Again, as in apostolic days, persecution turned out to the furtherance of the gospel. In a loathsome dungeon crowded with profligates and felons, John Bunyan breathed the very atmosphere of heaven; and there he wrote his wonderful allegory of the pilgrim's journey from the land of destruction to the celestial city. For over two hundred years that voice from Bedford jail has spoken with thrilling power to the hearts of men. Bunyan's *Pilgrim's Progress* and *Grace Abounding to the Chief of Sinners* have guided many feet into the path of life.

Baxter, Flavel, Alleine, and other men of talent, education, and deep Christian experience stood up in valiant defense of the faith which was once delivered to the saints. The work accomplished by these men, proscribed and outlawed by the rulers of this world, can never perish. Flavel's *Fountain of Life* and *Method of Grace* have taught thousands how to commit the keeping of their souls to Christ. Baxter's *Reformed Pastor* has proved a blessing to many who desire a revival of the work of God, and his *Saints' Everlasting Rest* has done its work in leading souls to the "rest" that remaineth for the people of God.

A hundred years later, in a day of great spiritual darkness, Whitefield and the Wesleys appeared as light bearers for God. Under the rule of the established church the people of England had lapsed into a state of religious declension hardly to be distinguished from heathenism. Natural religion was the favorite study of the clergy, and included most of their theology. The higher classes sneered at piety, and prided themselves on being above what they called its fanaticism. The lower classes were grossly ignorant and abandoned to vice, while the church had no courage or faith any longer to support the downfallen cause of truth.

The great doctrine of justification by faith, so clearly taught by Luther, had been almost wholly lost sight of; and the Romish principle of trusting to good works for salvation, had taken its place. Whitefield and the Wesleys, who were members of the established church, were sincere seekers for the favor of God, and this they had been taught was to be secured by a virtuous life and an observance of the ordinances of religion.

When Charles Wesley at one time fell ill, and anticipated that death was approaching, he was asked upon what he rested his hope of eternal life. His answer was: "I have used my best endeavors to serve God." As the friend who had put the question seemed not to be fully satisfied with his answer, Wesley thought: "What! are not my endeavors a sufficient ground of hope? Would he rob me of my endeavors? I have nothing else to trust to." —John Whitehead, *Life of the Rev. Charles Wesley*, page 102. Such was the dense darkness that had settled down on the church, hiding the atonement, robbing Christ of His glory, and turning the minds of men from their only hope of salvation—the blood of the crucified Redeemer.

Wesley and his associates were led to see that true religion is seated in the heart, and that God's law extends to the thoughts as well as to the words and actions. Convinced of the necessity of holiness of heart, as well as correctness of outward deportment, they set out in earnest upon a new life. By the most diligent and prayerful efforts they endeavored to subdue the evils of the natural heart. They lived a life of self-denial, charity, and humiliation, observing with great rigor and exactness every measure which they thought could be helpful to them in obtaining what they most desired—that holiness which could secure the favor of God. But they did not obtain the object which they sought. In vain were their endeavors to free themselves from the condemnation of sin or to break its power. It was the same struggle which Luther had experienced in his cell at Erfurt. It was the same question which had tortured his soul—"How should man be just before God?" Job. 9:2.

The fires of divine truth, well-nigh extinguished upon the altars of Protestantism, were to be rekindled from the ancient torch handed down the ages by the Bohemian Christians. After the Reformation, Protestantism in Bohemia had been trampled out by the hordes of Rome. All who refused to renounce the truth were forced to flee. Some of these, finding refuge in Saxony, there maintained the ancient faith. It was from the descendants of these Christians that light came to Wesley and his associates.

John and Charles Wesley, after being ordained to the ministry, were sent on a mission to America. On board the ship was a company of Moravians. Violent storms were encountered on the passage, and John Wesley, brought face to face with death, felt that he had not the assurance of peace with God. The Germans, on the contrary, manifested a calmness and trust to which he was a stranger.

"I had long before," he says, "observed the great seriousness of their behavior. Of their humility they had given a continual proof, by performing those servile offices for the other passengers which none of the English would undertake; for which they desired and would receive no pay, saying it was good for their proud hearts, and their loving Saviour had done more for them. And every day had given them occasion of showing a meekness which no injury could move. If they were pushed, struck, or thrown about, they rose again and went away; but no complaint was found in their mouth. There was now an opportunity of trying whether they were delivered from the spirit of fear, as well as from that of pride, anger, and revenge. In the midst of the psalm wherewith their service began, the sea broke over, split the mainsail in pieces, covered the ship, and poured in between the decks as if the great deep had already swallowed us up. A terrible screaming began among the English. The Germans calmly sang on. I asked one of them afterwards, 'Were you not afraid?' He answered, 'I thank God, no.' I asked, 'But were not your women and children afraid?' He replied mildly, 'No; our women and children are not afraid to die.'" —Whitehead, *Life of the Rev. John Wesley*, page 10.

Upon arriving in Savannah, Wesley for a short time abode with the Moravians, and was deeply impressed with their Christian deportment. Of one of their religious services, in striking contrast to the lifeless formalism of the Church of England, he wrote: "The great simplicity as well as solemnity of the whole almost made me forget the seventeen hundred years between, and imagine myself in one of those assemblies where form and state were not; but Paul, the tentmaker, or Peter, the fisherman, presided; yet with the demonstration of the Spirit and of power." —*Ibid.*, pages 11, 12.

On his return to England, Wesley, under the instruction of a Moravian preacher, arrived at a clearer understanding of Bible faith. He was convinced that he must renounce all dependence upon his own works for salvation and must trust wholly to "the Lamb of God, which taketh away the sin of the world." At a meeting of the Moravian society in London a statement was read from Luther, describing the change which the Spirit of God works in the heart of the believer. As Wesley listened, faith was kindled in his soul. "I felt my heart strangely warmed," he says. "I felt I did trust in Christ, Christ alone, for salvation: and an assurance was given me, that He had taken away *my* sins, even *mine*, and saved *me* from the law of sin and death." —*Ibid.*, page 52.

Through long years of wearisome and comfortless striving—years of rigorous self-denial, of reproach and humiliation—Wesley had steadfastly adhered to his one purpose of seeking God. Now he had found Him; and he found that the grace which he had toiled to win by prayers and fasts, by almsdeeds and self-abnegation, was a gift, "without money and without price."

Once established in the faith of Christ, his whole soul burned with the desire to spread everywhere a knowledge of the glorious gospel of God's free grace. "I look upon all the world as my parish," he said; "in whatever part of it I am, I judge it meet, right, and my bounden duty, to declare unto all that are willing to hear, the glad tidings of salvation." —*Ibid.*, page 74.

He continued his strict and self-denying life, not now as the *ground*, but the *result* of faith; not the *root*, but the *fruit* of holiness. The grace of God in Christ is the foundation of the Christian's hope, and that grace will be manifested in obedience. Wesley's life was devoted to the preaching of the great truths which he had received—justification through faith in the atoning blood of Christ, and the renewing power of the Holy Spirit upon the heart, bringing forth fruit in a life conformed to the example of Christ.

Whitefield and the Wesleys had been prepared for their work by long and sharp personal convictions of their own lost condition; and that they might be able to endure hardness as good soldiers of Christ, they had been subjected to the fiery ordeal of scorn, derision, and persecution, both in the university and as they were entering the ministry. They and a few others who sympathized with them were contemptuously called Methodists by their ungodly fellow students—a name which is at the present time regarded as honorable by one of the largest denominations in England and America.

As members of the Church of England they were strongly attached to her forms of worship, but the Lord had presented before them in His word a higher standard. The Holy Spirit urged them to preach Christ and Him crucified. The power of the Highest attended their labors. Thousands were convicted and truly converted. It was necessary that these sheep be protected from ravening wolves. Wesley had no thought of forming a new denomination, but he organized them under what was called the Methodist Connection.

Mysterious and trying was the opposition which these preachers encountered from the established church; yet God, in His wisdom, had overruled events to cause the reform to begin within the church itself. Had it come wholly from without, it would not have penetrated where it was so much needed. But as the revival preachers were churchmen, and labored within the pale of the church wherever they could find opportunity, the truth had an entrance where the doors would otherwise have remained closed. Some of the clergy were roused from their moral stupor and became zealous preachers in their own parishes. Churches that had been petrified by formalism were quickened into life.

In Wesley's time, as in all ages of the church's history, men of different gifts performed their appointed work. They did not harmonize upon every point of doctrine, but all were moved by the Spirit of God, and united in the absorbing aim to win souls to Christ. The differences between Whitefield and the Wesleys threatened at one time to create alienation; but as they learned meekness in the school of Christ, mutual forbearance and charity reconciled them. They had no time to dispute, while error and iniquity were teeming everywhere, and sinners were going down to ruin.

The servants of God trod a rugged path. Men of influence and learning employed their powers against them. After a time many of the clergy manifested determined hostility, and the doors of the churches were closed against a pure faith and those who proclaimed it. The course of the clergy in denouncing them from the pulpit aroused the elements of darkness, ignorance, and iniquity. Again and again did John Wesley escape death by a miracle of God's mercy. When the rage of the mob was excited against him, and there seemed no way of escape, an angel in human form came to his side, the mob fell back, and the servant of Christ passed in safety from the place of danger.

Of his deliverance from the enraged mob on one of these occasions, Wesley said: "Many endeavored to throw me down while we were going down hill on a slippery path to the town; as well judging that if I was once on the ground, I should hardly rise any more. But I made no stumble at all, nor the least slip, till I was entirely out of their hands. … Although many strove to lay hold on my collar or clothes, to pull me down, they could not fasten at all: only one got fast hold of the flap of my waistcoat, which was soon left in his hand; the other flap, in the pocket of which was a bank note, was torn but half off. … A lusty man just behind, struck at me several times, with a large oaken stick; with which if he had struck me once on the back part of my head, it would have saved him all further trouble. But every time, the blow was turned aside, I know not how; for I could not move to the right hand or left. … Another came rushing through the press, and raising his arm to strike, on a sudden let it drop, and only stroked my head, saying, 'What soft hair he has!' … The very first men whose hearts were turned were the heroes of the town, the captains of the rabble on all occasions, one of them having been a prize fighter at the bear gardens. …

"By how gentle degrees does God prepare us for His will! Two years ago, a piece of brick grazed my shoulders. It was a year after that the stone struck me between the eyes. Last month I received one blow, and this evening two, one before we came into the town, and one after we were gone out; but both were as nothing: for though one man struck me on the breast with all his might, and the other on the mouth with such force that the blood gushed out immediately, I felt no more pain from either of the blows than if they had touched me with a straw." —John Wesley, *Works*, vol. 3, pp. 297, 298.

The Methodists of those early days—people as well as preachers—endured ridicule and persecution, alike from church members and from the openly irreligious who were inflamed by their misrepresentations. They were arraigned before courts of justice—such only in name, for justice was rare in the courts of that time. Often they suffered violence from their persecutors. Mobs went from house to house, destroying furniture and goods, plundering whatever they chose, and brutally abusing men, women, and children. In some instances, public notices were posted, calling upon those who desired to assist in breaking the windows and robbing the houses of the Methodists, to assemble at a given time and place. These open violations of both human and divine law were allowed to pass without a reprimand. A systematic persecution was carried on against a people whose only fault was that of seeking to turn the feet of sinners from the path of destruction to the path of holiness.

Said John Wesley, referring to the charges against himself and his associates: "Some allege that the doctrines of these men are false, erroneous, and enthusiastic; that they are new and unheard-of till of late; that they are Quakerism, fanaticism, popery. This whole pretense has been already cut up by the roots, it having been shown at large that every branch of this doctrine is the plain doctrine of Scripture interpreted by our own church. Therefore it cannot be either false or erroneous, provided the Scripture be true." "Others allege, "Their doctrine is too strict; they make the way to heaven too narrow." And this is in truth the original objection, (as it was almost the only one for some time,) and is secretly at the bottom of a thousand more, which appear in various forms. But do they make the way to heaven any narrower than our Lord and His apostles made it? Is their doctrine stricter than that of the Bible? Consider only a few plain texts: 'Thou shalt love the Lord thy God with all thy heart, and with all thy mind, and with all thy soul, and with all thy strength.' 'For every idle word which men shall speak, they shall give an account in the day of judgment.' 'Whether ye eat, or drink, or whatever ye do, do all to the glory of God.'

"If their doctrine is stricter than this, they are to blame; but you know in your conscience it is not. And who can be one jot less strict without corrupting the word of God? Can any steward of the mysteries of God be found faithful if he change any part of that sacred depositum? No. He can abate nothing, he can soften nothing; he is constrained to declare to all men, 'I may not bring down the Scripture to your taste. You must come up to it, or perish forever.' This is the real ground of that other popular cry concerning 'the uncharitableness of these men.' Uncharitable, are they? In what respect? Do they not feed the hungry and clothe the naked? 'No; that is not the thing: they are not wanting in this: but they are so uncharitable in judging! they think none can be saved but those of their own way.'" —*Ibid.,* vol. 3, pp. 152, 153.

The spiritual declension which had been manifest in England just before the time of Wesley was in great degree the result of antinomian teaching. Many affirmed that Christ had abolished the moral law and that Christians are therefore under no obligation to observe it; that a believer is freed from the "bondage of good works." Others, though admitting the perpetuity of the law, declared that it was unnecessary for ministers to exhort the people to obedience of its precepts, since those whom God had elected to salvation would, "by the irresistible impulse of divine grace, be led to the practice of piety and virtue," while those who were doomed to eternal reprobation "did not have power to obey the divine law."

Others, also holding that "the elect cannot fall from grace nor forfeit the divine favor," arrived at the still more hideous conclusion that "the wicked actions they commit are not really sinful, nor to be considered as instances of their violation of the divine law, and that, consequently, they have no occasion either to confess their sins or to break them off by repentance." —McClintock and Strong, *Cyclopedia*, art. "Antinomians." Therefore, they declared that even one of the vilest of sins, "considered universally an enormous violation of the divine law, is not a sin in the sight of God," if committed by one of the elect, "because it is one of the essential and distinctive characteristics of the elect, that they cannot do anything that is either displeasing to God or prohibited by the law."

These monstrous doctrines are essentially the same as the later teaching of popular educators and theologians—that there is no unchangeable divine law as the standard of right, but that the standard of morality is indicated by society itself, and has constantly been subject to change. All these ideas are inspired by the same master spirit—by him who, even among the sinless inhabitants of heaven, began his work of seeking to break down the righteous restraints of the law of God.

The doctrine of the divine decrees, unalterably fixing the character of men, had led many to a virtual rejection of the law of God. Wesley steadfastly opposed the errors of the antinomian teachers and showed that this doctrine which led to antinomianism was contrary to the Scriptures. "The grace of God that bringeth salvation hath appeared to *all men.*" "This is good and acceptable in the sight of God our Saviour; who will have *all men* to be saved, and to come unto the knowledge of the truth. For there is one God, and one mediator between God and men, the man Christ Jesus; who gave Himself a ransom for *all.*" Titus 2:11; 1 Timothy 2:3-6. The Spirit of God is freely bestowed to enable every man to lay hold upon the means of salvation. Thus Christ, "the true Light," "lighteth every man that cometh into the world." John 1:9. Men fail of salvation through their own willful refusal of the gift of life.

In answer to the claim that at the death of Christ the precepts of the Decalogue had been abolished with the ceremonial law, Wesley said: "The moral law, contained in the Ten Commandments and enforced by the prophets, He did not take away. It was not the design of His coming to revoke any part of this. This is a law which never can be broken, which 'stands fast as the faithful witness in heaven.' ... This was from the beginning of the world, being 'written not on tables of stone,' but on the hearts of all the children of men, when they came out of the hands of the Creator. And however the letters once wrote by the finger of God are now in a great measure defaced by sin, yet can they not wholly be blotted out, while we have any consciousness of good and evil. Every part of this law must remain in force upon all mankind, and in all ages; as not depending either on time or place, or any other circumstances liable to change, but on the nature of God, and the nature of man, and their unchangeable relation to each other.

"'I am not come to destroy, but to fulfill.' ... Without question, His meaning in this place is (consistently with all that goes before and follows after),—I am come to establish it in its fullness, in spite of all the glosses of men: I am come to place in a full and clear view whatsoever was dark or obscure therein: I am come to declare the true and full import of every part of it; to show the length and breadth, the entire extent, of every commandment contained therein, and the height and depth, the inconceivable purity and spirituality of it in all its branches." —Wesley, sermon 25.

Wesley declared the perfect harmony of the law and the gospel. "There is, therefore, the closest connection that can be conceived, between the law and the gospel. On the one hand, the law continually makes way for, and points us to, the gospel; on the other, the gospel continually leads us to a more exact fulfilling of the law. The law, for instance, requires us to love God, to love our neighbor, to be meek, humble, or holy. We feel that we are not sufficient for these things; yea, that 'with man this is impossible;' but we see a promise of God to give us that love, and to make us humble, meek, and holy: we lay hold of this gospel, of these glad tidings; it is done unto us according to our faith; and 'the righteousness of the law is fulfilled in us,' through faith which is in Christ Jesus. ...

"In the highest rank of the enemies of the gospel of Christ," said Wesley, "are they who openly and explicitly 'judge the law' itself, and 'speak evil of the law;' who teach men to break (to dissolve, to loose, to untie the obligation of) not one only, whether of the least or of the greatest, but all the commandments at a stroke. ... The most surprising of all the circumstances that attend this strong delusion, is that they who are given up to it, really believe that they honor Christ by overthrowing His law, and that they are magnifying His office while they are destroying His doctrine! Yea, they honor Him just as Judas did when he said, 'Hail, Master, and kissed Him.' And He may as justly say to every one of them, 'Betrayest thou the Son of man with a kiss? It is no other than betraying Him with a kiss, to talk of His blood, and take away His crown; to set light by any part of His law, under pretense of advancing His gospel. Nor indeed can anyone escape this charge, who preaches faith in any such a manner as either directly or indirectly tends to set aside any branch of obedience: who preaches Christ so as to disannul, or weaken in any wise, the least of the commandments of God." —*Ibid.*

To those who urged that "the preaching of the gospel answers all the ends of the law," Wesley replied: "This we utterly deny. It does not answer the very first end of the law, namely, the convincing men of sin, the awakening those who are still asleep on the brink of hell." The apostle Paul declares that "by the law is the knowledge of sin;" "and not until man is convicted of sin, will he truly feel his need of the atoning blood of Christ. ... 'They that be whole,' as our Lord Himself observes, 'need not a physician, but they that are sick.' It is absurd, therefore, to offer a physician to them that are whole, or that at least imagine themselves so to be. You are first to convince them that they are sick; otherwise they will not thank you for your labor. It is equally absurd to offer Christ to them whose heart is whole, having never yet been broken." —*Ibid.,* sermon 35.

Thus while preaching the gospel of the grace of God, Wesley, like his Master, sought to "magnify the law, and make it honorable." Faithfully did he accomplish the work given him of God, and glorious were the results which he was permitted to behold. At the close of his long life of more than fourscore years—above half a century spent in itinerant ministry—his avowed adherents numbered more than half a million souls. But the multitude that through his labors had been lifted from the ruin and degradation of sin to a higher and a purer life, and the number who by his teaching had attained to a deeper and richer experience, will never be known till the whole family of the redeemed shall be gathered into the kingdom of God. His life presents a lesson of price-less worth to every Christian. Would that the faith and humility, the untiring zeal, self-sacrifice, and devotion of this servant of Christ might be reflected in the churches of today!

Nine

—The Bible and the French Revolution—

I n the sixteenth century the Reformation, presenting an open Bible to the people, had sought admission to all the countries of Europe. Some nations welcomed it with gladness, as a messenger of Heaven. In other lands the papacy succeeded to a great extent in preventing its entrance; and the light of Bible knowledge, with its elevating influences, was almost wholly excluded. In one country, though the light found entrance, it was not comprehended by the darkness. For centuries, truth and error struggled for the mastery. At last the evil triumphed, and the truth of Heaven was thrust out. "This is the condemnation, that light is come into the world, and men loved darkness rather than light." John 3:19. The nation was left to reap the results of the course which she had chosen. The restraint of God's Spirit was removed from a people that had despised the gift of His grace. Evil was permitted to come to maturity. And all the world saw the fruit of willful rejection of the light.

The war against the Bible, carried forward for so many centuries in France, culminated in the scenes of the Revolution. That terrible outbreaking was but the legitimate result of Rome's suppression of the Scriptures. It presented the most striking illustration which the world has ever witnessed of the working out of the papal policy—an illustration of the results to which for more than a thousand years the teaching of the Roman Church had been tending.

The suppression of the Scriptures during the period of papal supremacy was foretold by the prophets; and the Revelator points also to the terrible results that were to accrue especially to France from the domination of the "man of sin."

Said the angel of the Lord: "The holy city shall they tread underfoot forty and two months. And I will give power unto My two witnesses, and they shall prophesy a thousand two hundred and threescore days, clothed in sackcloth. ... And when they shall have finished their testimony, the beast that ascendeth out of the bottomless pit shall make war against them, and shall overcome them, and kill them. And their dead bodies shall lie in the street of the great city, which spiritually is called Sodom and Egypt, where also our Lord was crucified. ... And they that dwell upon the earth shall rejoice over them, and make merry, and shall send gifts one to another; because these two prophets tormented them that dwelt on the earth. And after three days and a half the Spirit of life from

God entered into them, and they stood upon their feet; and great fear fell upon them which saw them." Revelation 11:2-11.

The periods here mentioned—"forty and two months," and "a thousand two hundred and threescore days"—are the same, alike representing the time in which the church of Christ was to suffer oppression from Rome. The 1,260 years of papal supremacy began in A.D. 538, and would therefore terminate in 1798. At that time a French army entered Rome and made the pope a prisoner, and he died in exile. Though a new pope was soon afterward elected, the papal hierarchy has never since been able to wield the power which it before possessed.

The persecution of the church did not continue throughout the entire period of the 1,260 years. God in mercy to His people cut short the time of their fiery trial. In foretelling the "great tribulation" to befall the church, the Saviour said: "Except those days should be shortened, there should no flesh be saved: but for the elect's sake those days shall be shortened." Matthew 24:22. Through the influence of the Reformation the persecution was brought to an end prior to 1798.

Concerning the two witnesses the prophet declares further: "These are the two olive trees, and the two candlesticks standing before the God of the earth." "Thy word," said the psalmist, "is a lamp unto my feet, and a light unto my path." Revelation 11:4; Psalm 119:105. The two witnesses represent the Scriptures of the Old and the New Testament. Both are important testimonies to the origin and perpetuity of the law of God. Both are witnesses also to the plan of salvation. The types, sacrifices, and prophecies of the Old Testament point forward to a Saviour to come. The Gospels and Epistles of the New Testament tell of a Saviour who has come in the exact manner foretold by type and prophecy.

"They shall prophecy a thousand two hundred and threescore days, clothed in sackcloth." During the greater part of this period, God's witnesses remained in a state of obscurity. The papal power sought to hide from the people the word of truth, and set before them false witnesses to contradict its testimony. When the Bible was proscribed by religious and secular authority; when its testimony was perverted, and every effort made that men and demons could invent to turn the minds of the people from it; when those who dared proclaim its sacred truths were hunted, betrayed, tortured, buried in dungeon cells, martyred for their faith, or compelled to flee to mountain fastnesses, and to dens and caves of the earth—then the faithful witnesses prophesied in sackcloth. Yet they continued their testimony throughout the entire period of 1,260 years. In the darkest times there were faithful men who loved God's word and were jealous for His honor. To these loyal servants were given wisdom, power, and authority to declare His truth during the whole of this time.

"And if any man will hurt them, fire proceedeth out of their mouth, and devoureth their enemies: and if any man will hurt them, he must in this manner be killed." Revelation 11:5. Men cannot with impunity trample upon the word of God. The meaning of this fearful denunciation is set forth in the closing chapter of the Revelation: "I testify unto every man that heareth the words of the prophecy of this book, If any man shall add unto these things, God shall add unto him the plagues that are written in this book: and if any man shall take away from the words of the book of this prophecy, God shall take away his part out of the book of life, and out of the holy city, and from the things which are written in this book." Revelation 22:18, 19.

Such are the warnings which God has given to guard men against changing in any manner that which He has revealed or commanded. These solemn denunciations apply to all who by their influence lead men to regard lightly the law of God. They should cause those to fear and tremble who flippantly declare it a matter of little consequence whether we obey God's law or not. All who exalt their own opinions above divine revelation, all who would change the plain meaning of Scripture to suit their own convenience, or for the sake of conforming to the world, are taking upon themselves a fearful responsibility. The written word, the law of God, will measure the character of every man and condemn all whom this unerring test shall declare wanting.

"When they shall have finished [are finishing] their testimony." The period when the two witnesses were to prophesy clothed in sackcloth, ended in 1798. As they were approaching the termination of their work in obscurity, war was to be made upon them by the power represented as "the beast that ascendeth out of the bottomless pit." In many of the nations of Europe the powers that ruled in church and state had for centuries been controlled by Satan through the medium of the papacy. But here is brought to view a new manifestation of satanic power.

It had been Rome's policy, under a profession of reverence for the Bible, to keep it locked up in an unknown tongue and hidden away from the people. Under her rule the witnesses prophesied "clothed in sackcloth." But another power—the beast from the bottomless pit—was to arise to make open, avowed war upon the word of God.

"The great city" in whose streets the witnesses are slain, and where their dead bodies lie, is "spiritually" Egypt. Of all nations presented in Bible history, Egypt most boldly denied the existence of the living God and resisted His commands. No monarch ever ventured upon more open and highhanded rebellion against the authority of Heaven than did the king of Egypt. When the message was brought him by Moses, in the name of the Lord, Pharaoh proudly answered: "Who is Jehovah, that I should hearken unto His voice to let Israel go? I know not Jehovah, and moreover I will not let Israel go." Exodus 5:2, A.R.V. This is atheism, and the nation represented by Egypt would give voice to a similar denial of the claims of the living God and would manifest a like spirit of unbelief and defiance. "The great city" is also compared, "spiritually," to Sodom. The corruption of Sodom in breaking the law of God was especially manifested in licentiousness. And this sin was also to be a preeminent characteristic of the nation that should fulfill the specifications of this scripture.

According to the words of the prophet, then, a little before the year 1798 some power of satanic origin and character would rise to make war upon the Bible. And in the land where the testimony of God's two witnesses should thus be silenced, there would be manifest the atheism of the Pharaoh and the licentiousness of Sodom.

This prophecy has received a most exact and striking fulfillment in the history of France. During the Revolution, in 1793, "the world for the first time heard an assembly of men, born and educated in civilization, and assuming the right to govern one of the finest of the European nations, uplift their united voice to deny the most solemn truth which man's soul receives, and renounce unanimously the belief and worship of a Deity." —Sir Walter Scott, *Life of Napoleon*, vol. 1, ch. 17. "France is the only nation in the world concerning which the authentic record survives, that as a nation she lifted her hand in open rebellion against the Author of the universe. Plenty of blasphemers, plenty of infidels, there have been, and still continue to be, in England, Germany, Spain, and elsewhere; but France stands apart in the world's history as the single state which, by the decree of her Legislative Assembly, pronounced that there was no God, and of which the entire population of the capital, and a vast majority elsewhere, women as well as men, danced and sang with joy in accepting the announcement." —*Blackwood's Magazine*, November, 1870.

France presented also the characteristics which especially distinguished Sodom. During the Revolution there was manifest a state of moral debasement and corruption similar to that which brought destruction upon the cities of the plain. And the historian presents together the atheism and the licentiousness of France, as given in the prophecy: "Intimately connected with these laws affecting religion, was that which reduced the union of marriage—the most sacred engagement which human beings can form, and the permanence of which leads most strongly to the consolidation of society—to the state of a mere civil contract of a transitory character, which any two persons might engage in and cast loose at pleasure. ... If fiends had set themselves to work to discover a mode of most effectually destroying whatever is venerable, graceful, or permanent in domestic life, and of obtaining at the same time an assurance that the mischief which it was their object to create should be perpetuated from one generation to another, they could not have invented a more effectual plan than the degradation of marriage. ... Sophie Arnoult, an actress famous for the witty things she said, described the republican marriage as 'the sacrament of adultery.' " —Scott, vol. 1, ch. 17.

"Where also our Lord was crucified." This specification of the prophecy was also fulfilled by France. In no land had the spirit of enmity against Christ been more strikingly displayed. In no country had the truth encountered more bitter and cruel opposition. In the persecution which France had visited upon the confessors of the gospel, she had crucified Christ in the person of His disciples.

Century after century the blood of the saints had been shed. While the Waldenses laid down their lives upon the mountains of Piedmont "for the word of God, and for the testimony of Jesus Christ," similar witness to the truth had been borne by their brethren, the Albigenses of France. In the days of the Reformation its disciples had been put to death with horrible tortures. King and nobles, highborn women and delicate maidens, the pride and chivalry of the nation, had feasted their eyes upon the agonies of the martyrs of Jesus. The brave Huguenots, battling for those rights which the human heart holds most sacred, had poured out their blood on many a hard-fought field. The Protestants were counted as outlaws, a price was set upon their heads, and they were hunted down like wild beasts.

The "Church in the Desert," the few descendants of the ancient Christians that still lingered in France in the eighteenth century, hiding away in the mountains of the south, still cherished the faith of their fathers. As they ventured to meet by night on mountainside or lonely moor, they were chased by dragoons and dragged away to lifelong slavery in the galleys. The purest, the most refined, and the most intelligent of the French were chained, in horrible torture, amidst robbers and assassins. (See Wylie, b. 22, ch. 6.) Others, more mercifully dealt with, were shot down in cold blood, as, unarmed and helpless, they fell upon their knees in prayer. Hundreds of aged men, defenseless women, and innocent children were left dead upon the earth at their place of meeting. In traversing the mountainside or the forest, where they had been accustomed to assemble, it was not unusual to find "at every four paces, dead bodies dotting the sward, and corpses hanging suspended from the trees." Their country, laid waste with the sword, the ax, the fagot, "was converted into one vast, gloomy wilderness." "These atrocities were enacted ... in no dark age, but in the brilliant era of Louis XIV. Science was then cultivated, letters flourished, the divines of the court and of the capital were learned and eloquent men, and greatly affected the graces of meekness and charity." —*Ibid.*, b. 22, ch. 7.

But blackest in the black catalogue of crime, most horrible among the fiendish deeds of all the dreadful centuries, was the St. Bartholomew Massacre. The world still recalls with shuddering horror the scenes of that most cowardly and cruel onslaught. The king of France, urged on by Romish priests and prelates, lent his sanction to the dreadful work. A bell, tolling at dead of night, was a signal for the slaughter. Protestants by thousands, sleeping quietly in their homes, trusting to the plighted honor of their king, were dragged forth without a warning and murdered in cold blood.

As Christ was the invisible leader of His people from Egyptian bondage, so was Satan the unseen leader of his subjects in this horrible work of multiplying martyrs. For seven days the massacre was continued in Paris, the first three with inconceivable fury. And it was not confined to the city itself, but by special order of the king was extended to all the provinces and towns where Protestants were found. Neither age nor sex was respected. Neither the innocent babe nor the man of gray hairs was spared. Noble and peasant, old and young, mother and child, were cut down together. Throughout France the butchery continued for two months. Seventy thousand of the very flower of the nation perished.

"When the news of the massacre reached Rome, the exultation among the clergy knew no bounds. The cardinal of Lorraine rewarded the messenger with a thousand crowns; the cannon of St. Angelo thundered forth a joyous salute; and bells rang out from every steeple; bonfires turned night into day; and Gregory XIII, attended by the cardinals and other ecclesiastical dignitaries, went in long procession to the church of St. Louis, where the cardinal of Lorraine chanted a *Te Deum*. ... A medal was struck to commemorate the massacre, and in the Vatican may still be seen three frescoes of Vasari, describing the attack upon the admiral, the king in council plotting the massacre, and the massacre itself. Gregory sent Charles the Golden Rose; and four months after the massacre, ... he listened complacently to the sermon of a French priest, ... who spoke of 'that day so full of happiness and joy, when the most holy father received the news, and went in solemn state to render thanks to God and St. Louis.'" —Henry White, *The Massacre of St. Bartholomew*, ch. 14, par. 34.

The same master spirit that urged on the St. Bartholomew Massacre led also in the scenes of the Revolution. Jesus Christ was declared to be an impostor, and the rallying cry of the French infidels was, "Crush the Wretch," meaning Christ. Heaven-daring blasphemy and abominable wickedness went hand in hand, and the basest of men, the most abandoned monsters of cruelty and vice, were most highly exalted. In all this, supreme homage was paid to Satan; while Christ, in His characteristics of truth, purity, and unselfish love, was crucified.

"The beast that ascendeth out of the bottomless pit shall make war against them, and shall overcome them, and kill them." The atheistical power that ruled in France during the Revolution and the Reign of Terror, did wage such a war against God and His holy word as the world had never witnessed. The worship of the Deity was abolished by the National Assembly. Bibles were collected and publicly burned with every possible manifestation of scorn. The law of God was trampled underfoot. The institutions of the Bible were abolished. The weekly rest day was set aside, and in its stead every tenth day was devoted to reveling and blasphemy. Baptism and the Communion were prohibited. And announcements posted conspicuously over the burial places declared death to be an eternal sleep.

The fear of God was said to be so far from the beginning of wisdom that it was the beginning of folly. All religious worship was prohibited, except that of liberty and the country. The "constitutional bishop of Paris was brought forward to play the principal part in the most impudent and scandalous farce ever acted in the face of a national representation. ... He was brought forward in full procession, to declare to the Convention that the religion which he had taught so many years was, in every respect, a piece of priestcraft, which had no foundation either in history or sacred truth. He disowned, in solemn and explicit terms, the existence of the Deity to whose worship he had been consecrated, and devoted himself in future to the homage of liberty, equality, virtue, and morality. He then laid on the table his episcopal decorations, and received a fraternal embrace from the president of the Convention. Several apostate priests followed the example of this prelate." —Scott, vol. 1, ch. 17.

"And they that dwell upon the earth shall rejoice over them, and make merry, and shall send gifts one to another; because these two prophets tormented them that dwelt on the earth." Infidel France had silenced the reproving voice of God's two witnesses. The word of truth lay dead in her streets, and those who hated the restrictions and requirements of God's law were jubilant. Men publicly defied the King of heaven. Like the sinners of old, they cried: "How doth God know? and is there knowledge in the Most High?" Psalm 73:11.

With blasphemous boldness almost beyond belief, one of the priests of the new order said: "God, if You exist, avenge Your injured name. I bid You defiance! You remain silent; You dare not launch Your thunders. Who after this will believe in Your existence?" —Lacretelle, *History*, vol. 11, p. 309; in Sir Archibald Alison, *History of Europe*, vol. 1, ch. 10. What an echo is this of the Pharaoh's demand: "Who is Jehovah, that I should obey His voice?" "I know not Jehovah!"

"The fool hath said in his heart, There is no God." Psalm 14:1. And the Lord declares concerning the perverters of the truth: "Their folly shall be manifest unto all." 2 Timothy 3:9. After France had renounced the worship of the living God, "the high and lofty One that inhabiteth eternity," it was only a little time till she descended to degrading idolatry, by the worship of the Goddess of Reason, in the person of a profligate woman. And this in the representative assembly of the nation, and by its highest civil and legislative authorities! Says the historian: "One of the ceremonies of this insane time stands unrivaled for absurdity combined with impiety. The doors of the Convention were thrown open to a band of musicians, preceded by whom, the members of the municipal body entered in solemn procession, singing a hymn in praise of liberty, and escorting, as the object of their future worship, a veiled female, whom they termed the Goddess of Reason. Being brought within the bar, she was unveiled with great form, and placed on the right of the president, when she was generally recognized as a dancing girl of the opera. ...To this person, as the fittest representative of that reason whom they worshiped, the National Convention of France rendered public homage.

"This impious and ridiculous mummery had a certain fashion; and the installation of the Goddess of Reason was renewed and imitated throughout the nation, in such places where the inhabitants desired to show themselves equal to all the heights of the Revolution." —Scott, vol. 1, ch. 17.

Said the orator who introduced the worship of Reason: "Legislators! Fanaticism has given way to reason. Its bleared eyes could not endure the brilliancy of the light. This day an immense concourse has assembled beneath those gothic vaults, which, for the first time, re-echoed the truth. There the French have celebrated the only true worship,—that of Liberty, that of Reason. There we have formed wishes for the prosperity of the arms of the Republic. There we have abandoned inanimate idols for Reason, for that animated image, the masterpiece of nature." —M. A. Thiers, *History of the French Revolution*, vol. 2, pp. 370, 371.

When the goddess was brought into the Convention, the orator took her by the hand, and turning to the assembly said: "Mortals, cease to tremble before the powerless thunders of a God whom your fears have created. Henceforth acknowledge no divinity but Reason. I offer you its noblest and purest image; if you must have idols, sacrifice only to such as this. ... Fall before the august Senate of Freedom, oh! Veil of Reason!"

"The goddess, after being embraced by the president, was mounted on a magnificent car, and conducted, amid an immense crowd, to the cathedral of Notre Dame, to take the place of the Deity. There she was elevated on the high altar, and received the adoration of all present." —Alison, vol. 1, ch. 10.

This was followed, not long afterward, by the public burning of the Bible. On one occasion "the Popular Society of the Museum" entered the hall of the municipality, exclaiming, "*Vive la Raison!*" and carrying on the top of a pole the half-burned remains of several books, among others breviaries, missals, and the Old and New Testaments, which "expiated in a great fire," said the president, "all the fooleries which they have made the human race commit." —*Journal of Paris*, 1793, No. 318. Quoted in Buchez-Roux, *Collection of Parliamentary History*, vol. 30, pp. 200, 201.

It was popery that had begun the work which atheism was completing. The policy of Rome had wrought out those conditions, social, political, and religious, that were hurrying France on to ruin. Writers, in referring to the horrors of the Revolution, say that these excesses are to be charged upon the throne and the church. In strict justice they are to be charged upon the church. Popery had poisoned the minds of kings against the Reformation, as an enemy to the crown, an element of discord that would be fatal to the peace and harmony of the nation. It was the genius of Rome that by this means inspired the direst cruelty and the most galling oppression which proceeded from the throne.

The spirit of liberty went with the Bible. Wherever the gospel was received, the minds of the people were awakened. They began to cast off the shackles that had held them bondslaves of ignorance, vice, and superstition. They began to think and act as men. Monarchs saw it and trembled for their despotism.

Rome was not slow to inflame their jealous fears. Said the pope to the regent of France in 1525: "This mania [Protestantism] will not only confound and destroy religion, but all principalities, nobility, laws, orders, and ranks besides." —G. de Felice, *History of the Protestants of France*, b. 1, ch. 2, par. 8. A few years later a papal nuncio warned the king: "Sire, be not deceived. The Protestants will upset all civil as well as religious order. ... The throne is in as much danger as the altar. ... The introduction of a new religion must necessarily introduce a new government." —D'Aubigne, *History of the Reformation in Europe in the Time of Calvin*, b. 2, ch. 36. And theologians appealed to the prejudices of the people by declaring that the Protestant doctrine "entices men away to novelties and folly; it robs the king of the devoted affection of his subjects, and devastates both church and state." Thus Rome succeeded in arraying France against the Reformation. "It was to uphold the throne, preserve the nobles, and maintain the laws, that the sword of persecution was first unsheathed in France." —Wylie, b. 13, ch. 4.

Little did the rulers of the land foresee the results of that fateful policy. The teaching of the Bible would have implanted in the minds and hearts of the people those principles of justice, temperance, truth, equity, and benevolence which are the very cornerstone of a nation's prosperity. "Righteousness exalteth a nation." Thereby "the throne is established." Proverbs 14:34; 16:12. "The work of righteousness shall be peace;" and the effect, "quietness and assurance forever." Isaiah 32:17. He who obeys the divine law will most truly respect and obey the laws of his country. He who fears God will honor the king in the exercise of all just and legitimate authority. But unhappy France prohibited the Bible and banned its disciples. Century after century, men of principle and integrity, men of intellectual acuteness and moral strength, who had the courage to avow their convictions and the faith to suffer for the truth—for centuries these men toiled as slaves in the galleys, perished at the stake, or rotted in dungeon cells. Thousands upon thousands found safety in flight; and this continued for two hundred and fifty years after the opening of the Reformation.

"Scarcely was there a generation of Frenchmen during that long period that did not witness the disciples of the gospel fleeing before the insane fury of the persecutor, and carrying with them the intelligence, the arts, the industry, the order, in which, as a rule, they pre-eminently excelled, to enrich the lands in which they found an asylum. And in proportion as they replenished other countries with these good gifts, did they empty their own of them. If all that was now driven away had been retained in France; if, during these three hundred years, the industrial skill of the exiles had been cultivating her soil; if, during these three hundred years, their artistic bent had been improving her manufactures; if, during these three hundred years, their creative genius and analytic power had been enriching her literature and cultivating her science; if their wisdom had been guiding her councils, their bravery fighting her battles, their equity framing her laws, and the religion of the Bible strengthening the intellect and governing the conscience of her people, what a glory would at this day have encompassed France! What a great, prosperous, and happy country—a pattern to the nations—would she have been!

"But a blind and inexorable bigotry chased from her soil every teacher of virtue, every champion of order, every honest defender of the throne; it said to the men who would have made their country a 'renown and glory' in the earth, Choose which you will have, a stake or exile. At last the ruin of the state was complete; there remained no more conscience to be proscribed; no more religion to be dragged to the stake; no more patriotism to be chased into banishment." —Wylie, b. 13, ch. 20. And the Revolution, with all its horrors, was the dire result.

"With the flight of the Huguenots a general decline settled upon France. Flourishing manufacturing cities fell into decay; fertile districts returned to their native wildness; intellectual dullness and moral declension succeeded a period of unwonted progress. Paris became one vast almshouse, and it is estimated that, at the breaking out of the Revolution, two hundred thousand paupers claimed charity from the hands of the king. The Jesuits alone flourished in the decaying nation, and ruled with dreadful tyranny over churches and schools, the prisons and the galleys."

The gospel would have brought to France the solution of those political and social problems that baffled the skill of her clergy, her king, and her legislators, and finally plunged the nation into anarchy and ruin. But under the domination of Rome the people had lost the Saviour's blessed lessons of self-sacrifice and unselfish love. They had been led away from the practice of self-denial for the good of others. The rich had found no rebuke for their oppression of the poor, the poor no help for their servitude and degradation. The selfishness of the wealthy and powerful grew more and more apparent and oppressive. For centuries the greed and profligacy of the noble resulted in grinding extortion toward the peasant. The rich wronged the poor, and the poor hated the rich.

In many provinces the estates were held by the nobles, and the laboring classes were only tenants; they were at the mercy of their landlords and were forced to submit to their exhorbitant demands. The burden of supporting both the church and the state fell upon the middle and lower classes, who were heavily taxed by the civil authorities and by the clergy. "The pleasure of the nobles was considered the supreme law; the farmers and the peasants might starve, for aught their oppressors cared. ... The people were compelled at every turn to consult the exclusive interest of the landlord. The lives of the agricultural laborers were lives of incessant work and unrelieved misery; their complaints, if they ever dared to complain, were treated with insolent contempt. The courts of justice would always listen to a noble as against a peasant; bribes were notoriously accepted by the judges; and the merest caprice of the aristocracy had the force of law, by virtue of this system of universal corruption. Of the taxes wrung from the commonalty, by the secular magnates on the one hand, and the clergy on the other, not half ever found its way into the royal or episcopal treasury; the rest was squandered in profligate self-indulgence. And the men who thus impoverished their fellow subjects were themselves exempt from taxation, and entitled by law or custom to all the appointments of the state. The privileged classes numbered a hundred and fifty thousand, and for their gratification millions were condemned to hopeless and degrading lives."

The court was given up to luxury and profligacy. There was little confidence existing between the people and the rulers. Suspicion fastened upon all the measures of the government as designing and selfish. For more than half a century before the time of the Revolution the throne was occupied by Louis XV, who, even in those evil times, was distinguished as an indolent, frivolous, and sensual monarch. With a depraved and cruel aristocracy and an impoverished and ignorant lower class, the state financially embarrassed and the people exasperated, it needed no prophet's eye to foresee a terrible impending outbreak. To the warnings of his counselors the king was accustomed to reply: "Try to make things go on as long as I am likely to live; after my death it may be as it will." It was in vain that the necessity of reform was urged. He saw the evils, but had neither the courage nor the power to meet them. The doom awaiting France was but too truly pictured in his indolent and selfish answer, "After me, the deluge!"

By working upon the jealousy of the kings and the ruling classes, Rome had influenced them to keep the people in bondage, well knowing that the state would thus be weakened, and purposing by this means to fasten both rulers and people in her thrall. With farsighted policy she perceived that in order to enslave men effectually, the shackles must be bound upon their souls; that the surest way to prevent them from escaping their bondage was to render them incapable of freedom. A thousandfold more terrible than the physical suffering which resulted from her policy, was the moral degradation. Deprived of the Bible, and abandoned to the teachings of bigotry and selfishness, the people were shrouded in ignorance and superstition, and sunken in vice, so that they were wholly unfitted for self-government.

But the outworking of all this was widely different from what Rome had purposed. Instead of holding the masses in a blind submission to her dogmas, her work resulted in making them infidels and revolutionists. Romanism they despised as priestcraft. They beheld the clergy as a party to their oppression. The only god they knew was the god of Rome; her teaching was their only religion. They regarded her greed and cruelty as the legitimate fruit of the Bible, and they would have none of it.

Rome had misrepresented the character of God and perverted His requirements, and now men rejected both the Bible and its Author. She had required a blind faith in her dogmas, under the pretended sanction of the Scriptures. In the reaction, Voltaire and his associates cast aside God's word altogether and spread everywhere the poison of infidelity. Rome had ground down the people under her iron heel; and now the masses, degraded and brutalized, in their recoil from her tyranny, cast off all restraint. Enraged at the glittering cheat to which they had so long paid homage, they rejected truth and falsehood together; and mistaking license for liberty, the slaves of vice exulted in their imagined freedom.

At the opening of the Revolution, by a concession of the king, the people were granted a representation exceeding that of the nobles and the clergy combined. Thus the balance of power was in their hands; but they were not prepared to use it with wisdom and moderation. Eager to redress the wrongs they had suffered, they determined to undertake the reconstruction of society. An outraged populace, whose minds were filled with bitter and long-treasured memories of wrong, resolved to revolutionize the state of misery that had grown unbearable and to avenge themselves upon those whom they regarded as the authors of their sufferings. The oppressed wrought out the lesson they had learned under tyranny and became the oppressors of those who had oppressed them.

Unhappy France reaped in blood the harvest she had sown. Terrible were the results of her submission to the controlling power of Rome. Where France, under the influence of Romanism, had set up the first stake at the opening of the Reformation, there the Revolution set up its first guillotine. On the very spot where the first martyrs to the Protestant faith were burned in the sixteenth century, the first victims were guillotined in the eighteenth. In repelling the gospel, which would have brought her healing, France had opened the door to infidelity and ruin. When the restraints of God's law were cast aside, it was found that the laws of man were inadequate to hold in check the powerful tides of human passion; and the nation swept on to revolt and anarchy. The war against the Bible inaugurated an era which stands in the world's history as the Reign of Terror. Peace and happiness were banished from the homes and hearts of men. No one was secure. He who triumphed today was suspected, condemned, tomorrow. Violence and lust held undisputed sway.

King, clergy, and nobles were compelled to submit to the atrocities of an excited and maddened people. Their thirst for vengeance was only stimulated by the execution of the king; and those who had decreed his death soon followed him to the scaffold. A general slaughter of all suspected of hostility to the Revolution was determined. The prisons were crowded, at one time containing more than two hundred thousand captives. The cities of the kingdom were filled with scenes of horror. One party of revolutionists was against another party, and France became a vast field for contending masses, swayed by the fury of their passions. "In Paris one tumult succeeded another, and the citizens were divided into a medley of factions, that seemed intent on nothing but mutual extermination." And to add to the general misery, the nation became involved in a prolonged and devastating war with the great powers of Europe. "The country was nearly bankrupt, the armies were clamoring for arrears of pay, the Parisians were starving, the provinces were laid waste by brigands, and civilization was almost extinguished in anarchy and license."

All too well the people had learned the lessons of cruelty and torture which Rome had so diligently taught. A day of retribution at last had come. It was not now the disciples of Jesus that were thrust into dungeons and dragged to the stake. Long ago these had perished or been driven into exile. Unsparing Rome now felt the deadly power of those whom she had trained to delight in deeds of blood. "The example of persecution which the clergy of France had exhibited for so many ages, was now retorted upon them with signal vigor. The scaffolds ran red with the blood of the priests. The galleys and the prisons, once crowded with Huguenots, were now filled with their persecutors. Chained to the bench and toiling at the oar, the Roman Catholic clergy experienced all those woes which their church had so freely inflicted on the gentle heretics."

"Then came those days when the most barbarous of all codes was administered by the most barbarous of all tribunals; when no man could greet his neighbors or say his prayers … without danger of committing a capital crime; when spies lurked in every corner; when the guillotine was long and hard at work every morning; when the jails were filled as close as the holds of a slave ship; when the gutters ran foaming with blood into the Seine. … While the daily wagonloads of victims were carried to their doom through the streets of Paris, the proconsuls, whom the sovereign committee had sent forth to the departments, reveled in an extravagance of cruelty unknown even in the capital. The knife of the deadly machine rose and fell too slow for their work of slaughter. Long rows of captives were mowed down with grapeshot. Holes were made in the bottom of crowded barges. Lyons was turned into a desert. At Arras even the cruel mercy of a speedy death was denied to the prisoners. All down the Loire, from Saumur to the sea, great flocks of crows and kites feasted on naked corpses, twined together in hideous embraces. No mercy was shown to sex or age. The number of young lads and of girls of seventeen who were murdered by that execrable government, is to be reckoned by hundreds. Babies torn from the breast were tossed from pike to pike along the Jacobin ranks." In the short space of ten years, multitudes of human beings perished.

All this was as Satan would have it. This was what for ages he had been working to secure. His policy is deception from first to last, and his steadfast purpose is to bring woe and wretchedness upon men, to deface and defile the workmanship of God, to mar the divine purposes of benevolence and love, and thus cause grief in heaven. Then by his deceptive arts he blinds the minds of men, and leads them to throw back the blame of his work upon God, as if all this misery were the result of the Creator's plan. In like manner, when those who have been degraded and brutalized through his cruel power achieve their freedom, he urges them on to excesses and atrocities. Then this picture of unbridled license is pointed out by tyrants and oppressors as an illustration of the results of liberty.

When error in one garb has been detected, Satan only masks it in a different disguise, and multitudes receive it as eagerly as at the first. When the people found Romanism to be a deception, and he could not through this agency lead them to transgression of God's law, he urged them to regard all religion as a cheat, and the Bible as a fable; and, casting aside the divine statutes, they gave themselves up to unbridled iniquity.

The fatal error which wrought such woe for the inhabitants of France was the ignoring of this one great truth: that true freedom lies within the proscriptions of the law of God. "O that thou hadst hearkened to My commandments! then had thy peace been as a river, and thy righteousness as the waves of the sea." "There is no peace, saith the Lord, unto the wicked." "But whoso hearkeneth unto Me shall dwell safely, and shall be quiet from fear of evil." Isaiah 48:18, 22; Proverbs 1:33.

Atheists, infidels, and apostates oppose and denounce God's law; but the results of their influence prove that the well-being of man is bound up with his obedience of the divine statutes. Those who will not read the lesson from the book of God are bidden to read it in the history of nations.

When Satan wrought through the Roman Church to lead men away from obedience, his agency was concealed, and his work was so disguised that the degradation and misery which resulted were not seen to be the fruit of transgression. And his power was so far counteracted by the working of the Spirit of God that his purposes were prevented from reaching their full fruition. The people did not trace the effect to its cause and discover the source of their miseries. But in the Revolution the law of God was openly set aside by the National Council. And in the Reign of Terror which followed, the working of cause and effect could be seen by all.

When France publicly rejected God and set aside the Bible, wicked men and spirits of darkness exulted in their attainment of the object so long desired—a kingdom free from the restraints of the law of God. Because sentence against an evil work was not speedily executed, therefore the heart of the sons of men was "fully set in them to do evil." Ecclesiastes 8:11. But the transgression of a just and righteous law must inevitably result in misery and ruin. Though not visited at once with judgments, the wickedness of men was nevertheless surely working out their doom. Centuries of apostasy and crime had been treasuring up wrath against the day of retribution; and when their iniquity was full, the despisers of God learned too late that it is a fearful thing to have worn out the divine patience. The restraining Spirit of God, which imposes a check upon the cruel power of Satan, was in a great measure removed, and he whose only delight is the wretchedness of men was permitted to work his will. Those who had chosen the service of rebellion were left to reap its fruits until the land was filled with crimes too horrible for pen to trace. From devastated provinces and ruined cities a terrible cry was heard—a cry of bitterest anguish. France was shaken as if by an earthquake. Religion, law, social order, the family, the state, and the church—all were smitten down by the impious hand that had been lifted against the law of God. Truly spoke the wise man: "The wicked shall fall by his own wickedness." "Though a sinner do evil a hundred times, and his days be prolonged, yet surely I know that it shall be well with them that fear God, which fear before Him: but it shall not be well with the wicked." Proverbs 11:5; Ecclesiastes 8:12, 13. "They hated knowledge, and did not choose the fear of the Lord;" "therefore shall they eat of the fruit of their own way, and be filled with their own devices." Proverbs 1:29, 31.

God's faithful witnesses, slain by the blasphemous power that "ascendeth out of the bottomless pit," were not long to remain silent. "After three days and a half the Spirit of life from God entered into them, and they stood upon their feet; and great fear fell upon them which saw them." Revelation 11:11. It was in 1793 that the decrees which abolished the Christian religion and set aside the Bible passed the French Assembly. Three years and a half later a resolution rescinding these decrees, thus granting toleration to the Scriptures, was adopted by the same body. The world stood aghast at the enormity of guilt which had resulted from a rejection of the Sacred Oracles, and men recognized the necessity of faith in God and His word as the foundation of virtue and morality. Saith the Lord: "Whom hast thou reproached and blasphemed? and against whom hast thou exalted thy voice, and lifted up thine eyes on high? even against the Holy One of Israel." Isaiah 37:23. "Therefore, behold, I will cause them to know, this once will I cause them to know My hand and My might; and they shall know that My name is Jehovah." Jeremiah 16:21, A.R.V.

Concerning the two witnesses the prophet declares further: "And they heard a great voice from heaven saying unto them, Come up hither. And they ascended up to heaven in a cloud; and their enemies beheld them." Revelation 11:12. Since France made war upon God's two witnesses, they have been honored as never before. In 1804 the British and Foreign Bible Society was organized. This was followed by similar organizations, with numerous branches, upon the continent of Europe. In 1816 the American Bible Society was founded. When the British Society was formed, the Bible had been printed and circulated in fifty tongues. It has since been translated into many hundreds of languages and dialects.

For the fifty years preceding 1792, little attention was given to the work of foreign missions. No new societies were formed, and there were but few churches that made any effort for the spread of Christianity in heathen lands. But toward the close of the eighteenth century a great change took place. Men became dissatisfied with the results of rationalism and realized the necessity of divine revelation and experimental religion. From this time the work of foreign missions attained an unprecedented growth.

The improvements in printing have given an impetus to the work of circulating the Bible. The increased facilities for communication between different countries, the breaking down of ancient barriers of prejudice and national exclusiveness, and the loss of secular power by the pontiff of Rome have opened the way for the entrance of the word of God. For some years the Bible has been sold without restraint in the streets of Rome, and it has now been carried to every part of the habitable globe.

The infidel Voltaire once boastingly said: "I am weary of hearing people repeat that twelve men established the Christian religion. I will prove that one man may suffice to overthrow it." Generations have passed since his death. Millions have joined in the war upon the Bible. But it is so far from being destroyed, that where there were a hundred in Voltaire's time, there are now ten thousand, yes, a hundred thousand copies of the book of God. In the words of an early Reformer concerning the Christian church, "The Bible is an anvil that has worn out many hammers." Saith the Lord: "No weapon that is formed against thee shall prosper; and every tongue that shall rise against thee in judgment thou shalt condemn." Isaiah 54:17.

"The word of our God shall stand forever." "All His commandments are sure. They stand fast for ever and ever, and are done in truth and uprightness." Isaiah 40:8; Psalm 111:7, 8. Whatever is built upon the authority of man will be overthrown; but that which is founded upon the rock of God's immutable word shall stand forever.